Orville Wheeler

My Jewsharp

Poems

Orville Wheeler

My Jewsharp
Poems

ISBN/EAN: 9783744710725

Printed in Europe, USA, Canada, Australia, Japan

Cover: Foto ©Thomas Meinert / pixelio.de

More available books at **www.hansebooks.com**

MY JEWSHARP;

OR,

POEMS,

BY

ORVILLE GOULD WHEELER.

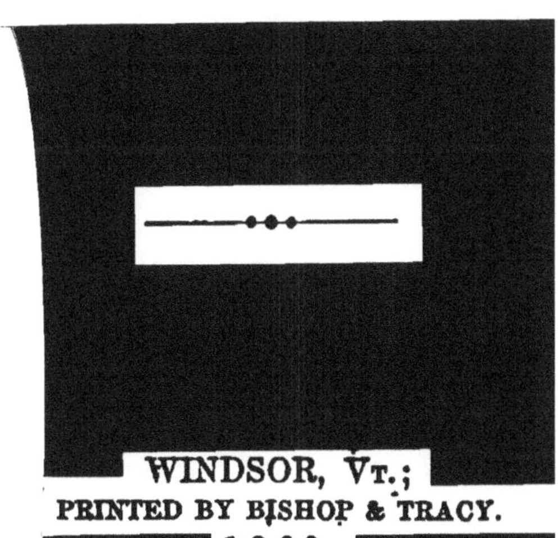

WINDSOR, VT.;
PRINTED BY BISHOP & TRACY.
1860.

CONTENTS.

MISCELLANEOUS.

SEMI-CENTENNIAL.

DELIVERED BEFORE THE

ASSOCIATED ALUMNI OF THE UNIVERSITY OF VERMONT, AUGUST 1, 1854,

SEMI-CENTENNIAL.

SINCE Ancient Bards, with brightest garlands crowned,
Were ever at the feet of Muses found,
And no one sings, in this our modern time,
Who does not first to old Parnassus climb,
Presumptuous would it be for me to dare,
Without at least a timid, trembling prayer,
Attempt the humblest flight, or breathe a strain,
Of which a mother e'en would not complain.
So flying from the busy haunts of men,
I sought the wild-wood shade, and sought it when
The hour was tranquil, and the sky serene,—
When, mingled with the variegated green,

The sunbeams, stealing through the waving trees,
Glanced from the leaves, that trembled in the breeze.

There, on a mossy knoll I laid my head,
And stretched my body on a leafy bed,
And sweetly summoned every wandering thought,
Ere yet the silent prayer my spirit wrought.

Oh, passing pleasant was it there to lie,
And see how lightly lay the floating sky,
A veil of azure o'er as bright a green
As e'er by nymph or sylvan Goddess seen,
As with the silken leaves, in dalliance soft,
The loving breezes played; so turned I oft,
And, 'mid the sunlight, scattered all around,
I watched their shadows playing on the ground.
The birds had either sought some other spot,
Or were asleep, for ne'er was gloomy grot
More silent than my cool and still retreat,
And silence for my purpose then was meet.

With such a velvet pillow for my head,
With such a leafy cushion for my bed,
Such beauty bending o'er me from above,
Such kisses from the breezes that I love,
How could a mortal in a better frame
The graceful Sisters woo, their favor claim?

The trembler thus began—"O sacred Nine!
O gentle, generous Sisterhood Divine!
Upon your humble worshipper O deign
To smile, or else all effort will be vain——"
But hark! what music floats upon the air?
So soon has come an answer to my prayer?
As softly swells the low Æolian strain,
It nearer comes, and thrills my throbbing brain;
It ceases—and I feel upon my brow
The feet of Fairies tripping o'er it now.

Zounds! what a thrust was that—with vile descent,
The rascal's on my precious blood intent.

A blow succeeds, that nearly splits the skull,
And strikes my raving, reeling senses dull,
And see, amid the multitude of foes,
That pendant spider steering for my nose,
And, O, beneath me all is crawling life,
And all engaged in most malicious strife,
Which may torment the raving Tyro most,
Of all that hungry, thirsty, bloody host.

Away I flew, and scarcely looked behind,
Henceforth to music deaf, to beauty blind,—
Such music as in summer forest sounds,
Such beauty as in summer wood abounds.

'Tis easy preaching, but to practise hard;
'Tis passing easy, for the dreamy Bard,
To paint yon rural scenes, and tell how sweet
To plunge within the sheltering retreat,
And there commune with Nature unadorned,
In simple beauty clad; but, O be warned!

And fail not, if the Muses you would woo,
The treacherous wood forever to eschew.

I sought the shore, and watched the restless waves,
As on they came, and o'er each other's graves
Remorseless rolled, as living mortals spread
Oblivion o er the memories of the dead.
It was an almost level, pebbly shore,
And yet, as on the raging billows pour,
Their crests, just now so angry, melt away,
Just kiss their pebbly bound, their tribute pay,
And, dying, sink beneath the troubled deep,
Where, buried, all their predecessors sleep.

So, too, the Living Masses roll along,
And though you scarce would think the rushing throng
Would find a barrier strong enough to stay
The multitudes that press the crowded way,
Yet still they yield, whene'er they reach the shore,
And, sinking, crowd the tide of life no more.

I weary wandered, with indifferent aim,
Until upon a different shore I came,—
No gentle margin, wooing to entrap
The sleepy wavelet, rolling in its lap,
But bold and steep the craggy rocks arose,
That frowned e'en when the waves were in repose;
If e'er they smile, 'tis when they keep at bay,
And dash the proudest billows into spray.

The winds were tired then, and merely rocked to sleep
The waves upon the bosom of the deep,
I smiled to see how lovingly caressed,
How kindly too, the old gray rocks were pressed;
A little while ago, how fiercely blew
The wrathful tempest, and how angry grew
The foaming waters,—lifting high their crest,
In fury plunging 'gainst the rocky breast,
But now they, creeping, strangely unabashed,
Caress the bosom they so lately lashed.

'Tis thus the child by foolish passion tossed,
Whene'er its proud, rebellious will is crossed,
Contends with "might and main" against her power,
Upon whose brow no angry tempests lower,
Subdued, it nestles in its mother's arms,
Who smiles away its anger and alarms.

Thus, too, when children of a larger growth
Contend against some heaven-descended Truth,
And foam and rage and vainly spend their breath
To crush the Life of that which knows not Death,—
And soon as e'er they find their weakness out,
And all their forces put to utter rout,
In fond embraces opposition ends,
And they're the most devoted of its friends.

Thus, too, in Congress Hall, beneath the dome,
An old man stood, amid the lashing foam
Of angry waters, ready to o'erwhelm

The Hero, but no Pilot at the helm
Was ever calmer, 'mid the howling storm,
Than was that "old man eloquent," whose form
Was bending 'neath the weight of four score years,
Whose Patriot blood had never freighted fears.
He conquered,—and all honor vied to give
The man who "ceased at once to work and live."

With evergreens those rocks are always crowned,
No fading foliage there is ever found,
A fitting, comely covering are they,
The ever-green upon the ever-gray.

I mused awhile among their solemn shades,
And thought, at times, I heard the coyish maids,
Folding their wings, a word of hope to speak ;—
O yes, I thought I felt upon my cheek
Their balmy breath, and strange, peculiar fire
Began my aching bosom to inspire.

'T was all a mockery,—the lulling breeze
Was only sighing 'mong the cedar trees,
And, now and then, was playing with my locks,
As, in despair, I sank upon the rocks.
So sweetly will the hand of love caress,
And soothingly your throbbing temples press,
Or fan your brow, and woo for you repose,
While kisses soft your weary eyelids close.

I slept, and, as the fashion is, I dreamed,—
Within a circle silently I seemed
Patient to wait for gentle spirit raps,
Hoping some kind old Grecian Bard, perhaps,
Or Roman,—Homer, Virgil, any one,—
Whose work on earth with honor had been done,
(If Ancient Poets, whirling in the "Spheres,"
Had soared too high to bend to mortal ears,)
A Shakspeare, Old John Milton, Walter Scott,
Might use their leisure hours, as well as not,

Communicating numbers through my pen,
That thus the world might hear them sing again.

How still that circle! Aye, like statues, still!
We heard the electric current of the will,
And Fancies trooping in their airy trains,—
And e'en the blood that rippled in our veins:
Our hearts would fain their timid beating stop,
Or start if truant pins presumed to drop;
Our thoughts with hopes and fears were strangely
mixed,
While all our eyes were on the table fixed.
It was an ancient table, and had borne
Many a fragrant feast, though now forlorn,
And merry voices oft had mingled there,
When hungry men did something else but stare.
Besides, 't was darkly hinted that, in times
Of old, bright spirits from the fairest climes,
And spirits which could warm the coldest blood,
Upon that table, visible, had stood.

We looked and listened, till three little raps,
That seemed like gentle baby-finger taps,
Announced the lucky man, the medium said,
To be myself, to whom the honored dead
Would graciously communicate a song;
Nor did I in amazement linger long,
But, pen on paper placed, I gave my hand
All to the guidance of the spirit-land.

My senses bound by strange magnetic spell,
What followed then, I cannot certain tell,—
But, when aroused, I sought the glowing page,
And hieroglyphics of a distant age
Found scattered o'er the spirit-scribbled sheet,
I thought no triumph ever more complete.
Alas for such as borrowed glory seek!
'T was either Choctaw or forgotten Greek.

Ah! whither, whither now shall I resort,
Of muse and spirit both the cruel sport?

Must I the path of Poesy forsake?
To dull and vulgar Prose again betake?
Just then, I felt a hand upon my arm,
So strangely fond, it had a magic charm,
Rekindled hope, and banished my despair,
It seemed to me a MOTHER'S hand was there.

I looked, and, looking, every nerve was thrilled,
And every ruffled passion, too, was stilled,
Our Alma Mater smiled upon her son,
And cheered the Heart that early she had won.
Of stature perfect, and of gracious mien,
A wreath upon her temples, wove of evergreen,
The olden bloom was still upon her face,
Of youth the beauty, and of age the grace,—
And still that same serene and quiet light
Of long ago, so pleasant and so bright.

"Arise," she said, "and let thy heart be cheered,
The appointed task is nothing to be feared,

Only a simple family affair.
Thy scattered Brothers will be gathered there,
Who will not come with cold Reviewer's ear,
Nor look on thee with heartless critic's leer.
Oh, no, as 'round the homestead they shall throng,
They only ask of thee a little homely song,
Withdraw thy straining, dim, near-sighted eyes,
Nor look so eager toward the far-off skies ;
Let Greeks degenerate guard Parnassus' Mount,
And soldiers drink from the old Castalian fount,—
If climb you will some dizzy, cloudy height,
To Camel's Hump betake your airy flight ;
Along your path you'll find as sweet a spring
As ever helped the Ancient Poet sing.
O'er fifty years, which have so quickly fled,
What sweet, sad memories are thickly spread,
Let them the burden of your numbers be,
Content if I but kindly smile on thee."

So, Brothers, here I cheerful come,
  Nor your forgiveness ask,
For since we now are all at Home,
  This is a pleasant task.
If strangers should my simple verse deride,
Enough, if you are smiling at their side.

And if indeed there were a frown
  To gather on your face,
Our sisters here would smile it down,
  With Charity's sweet grace.
Cheering the light the scattered groups display,
As clustering jewels of the milky way.

Not often do so many meet
  Around our classic hearth,
Not often here each other greet,
  In sadness and in mirth.
A strange commixture, sorrow, love and joy,
The white-haired Brother, and the dimpled Boy.

And Fathers, too, are gathered here,
Who, as my story runs,
Will find that they, 't is very clear,
Are Brothers to their Sons.
A curious, tangled web of gentle ties
Is wove, as Life's swift shuttle flies.

Indeed, whoever had a spot,
Known by the sweetest name,
A palace or the humblest cot,
And thither fondly came,
On some sweet festival, discovered there,
Beside the glossy curls, the silvered hair!

O yes, and childhood's laughing eyes
On Elder Brother gazed,
And listened with a strange surprise,
Confounded and amazed,
To hear him call on Mother by the same
Delightful, fond, endearing name.

Such seasons, too, will oft awake
Forgotten Harmonies.
When ashes of the Past we rake,
Conflicting memories
Come swiftly flying from the checquered ground,
And smiles of tears are oft the channels found.

From festive board, where mirthful songs
Are warbled with delight,
Where laughter light to merry jest belongs,
And all is fair and bright,
They hie them to some silent burial place,
Where darkly sleeps some well-remembered face.

From these familiar scenes our feet
Have, Brothers, distant strayed,
The years have fled, with wings how fleet,
Since first of us were made
Proud Bachelors, who eager then to win,
Were ready Life's great Battle to begin.

And yet these years, so quickly past,
Have whitened many a head,
And, Brothers, we are filling fast
The mansions of the dead.
The tombstone leans o'er many an early grave,
Where sleep the lost, the beautiful and brave.

And even on the very verge
Of this sweet festival,
We seem to hear the funeral dirge,
We seem to see the pall
That draped the bier of one, whose youthful head
Untimely slumbers with the countless dead.

One class has no one here to-day
To join the festive throng,
Its names are starred, and so are they,—
They have been sleeping long.
The gifted Brush, and Taylor pure and good,
We miss them from our pleasant Brotherhood.

How easy is it to recall
The forms familiar, dear,
Of many whom the funeral pall
Forbids to meet us here!
Perhaps their spirits hover o'er us now.
And wonder why a cloud is on our brow.

And some in far, far distant lands
Are spending brightest youth,
With noble missionary bands
Are toiling for the Truth;
Though perils in their thorny pathway lurk,
They cannot leave their Heaven-appointed work.

We gather from the sunny south,
Where bright Magnolias bloom,
Where Freedom shuts her honest mouth,
As closely as the tomb;
Where children almost curse the Father's graves
For leaving them a heritage of slaves.

We gather from the mighty West,
Where Prairie Oceans roll,
To all the world the region blest,
A refuge for the whole;—
Oh, yes, from South, from West, from East, from North,
Our Alma Mater calls her children forth.

The Lawyer drops his budding brief,
And leaves his cause to fate;
The Politician seeks relief
From heavy cares of State;
Doctors for once forsake their growing bill,
While Nature, unembarrassed, does her will.

The Farmer quits his patent plough,
Tired of experiment,
His jeering neighbors wondering how
The sage can pay his rent;
Their beaten paths his wisdom oft has crossed,
They therefore think his life in college lost.

The Merchant leaves his costly wares
To slumber on the shelf,
Or heaps, perhaps, his honest cares
Upon his other self;
Of course, although a Bachelor of Arts,
From him no simple customer e'er smarts.

The Clergy leave their loving flocks,
Forgetting for to-day
The number of the stumbling-blocks
That hedge their weary way;
They think the Real wondrous contrast bears
With bright Ideals, which of old were theirs.

Forgive, if in a single place
My muse be personal.
A Brother of the oldest class
Has proved perennial;
The younger Pilgrims, suffered here to meet,
His cordial welcome never fails to greet.

'T is pleasant, when we hither come,
And stranger faces find,
To have a Brother still at home,
So courteous and kind;
In learning wise, in social battle brave,
Long may the veteran, our Brother Adams, wave.

We even almost envy him,
On such a day as this,
For joyous are the tears that dim,
Mid this unusual bliss;
It would have been a privilege to stand
And see *those Brothers* grasp each other's hand.

How many tales have they to tell
Of cherished long ago!
Emotions strange their bosoms swell,
And tears, perhaps, do flow;
How they have changed, since they were happy boys,
And mingled here their labors and their joys!

The world has many changes seen,
Since first, on yonder Hill,
Of College dome the glittering sheen
Did scholar bosoms thrill.
Tyrants have mangled nations swallowed up;
Of vengeance, some have drunk the bitter cup.

Gay France has turned, t' amuse the world,
Many a somerset,
And monarchs from their thrones has hurled,
Whenever in a pet.
Her crown chameleon changes color oft,—
Malicious people think it covers something soft.

And yet upon her bloody soil
The bravest heroes grow,
As 'mid the serpent's quivering coil
The finest blossoms blow;
Her Bonaparte, of mightiest renown,
It took the World to haul his banner down.

Hungary bold has tried to gain
  Her rightful liberty,
While England saw, with cold disdain,
  The Czar enslave the free;
Her selfish silence now she pays with blood,
Her treasure wastes to stem the Cossack flood.

O, what surpassing eloquence
  That dying nation breathed!
Her Son, by darkest Providence,
  With brightest glory wreathed;
A sweeter voice the nations never heard,—
They listened, but returned no cheering word.

And Italy, poor Italy,
  The cherished Home of Art,
Presumed, in her simplicity,
  The world would take her part;
But honest France, a red Republic then,
Her Freemen sent, to guard the Tyrant's den.

Poland has sunk, to rise no more,
In blood her sun has set,
In vain her sons for help implore—
Their cries with mockery met;
Surrounding Despots crown the dismal tale,
And rob her realm to hush her dying wail.

Our Country, too, has whirled along
The track of destiny,
Events her brilliant record throng,
Of thrilling memory;
Dear Country! would that we could think of thee,
An undefiled, sweet Land of Liberty.

But there are shadows on the Moon,
And spots upon the Sun,—
Perhaps it is as yet too soon,
(Our race is just begun,)
Too soon for Earth to turn to Heaven a spot
So clear, so bright, without a single blot.

Thirteen enfeebled, wasted States
Have grown to thirty-one,
And still we 're rushing toward the gates
Where sleeps the setting sun;
Who cares? if Freedom keeps an equal pace,
Commending thus our Land to Heaven's grace.

Our Franklin first the Lightning caught,
Bridling the fiery steed,
But Morse the subtle courser taught
Along the wires to speed;
Now, safely harnessed to the car of thought,
The greatest wonders of the Age are wrought.

When these men * gazed from College Hill
They saw the vessel frail
Obey the fickle breeze's will,
And spread the timid sail;
But now the gorgeous steamer plows the wave,
Heedless of how the angry Tempests rave.

* Our Elder Brothers.

Stage coaches then, at early dawn,
Did sleepy travellers waken,
Retired now, their glory gone,
Like fallen friends, forsaken;
A half-tamed Demon, some have called him Horse,
Now rushes madly o'er the iron course.

His horrid screech has scared the Stag,
To wildest valleys fled,
The eagle from his mountain crag
Has heard his thundering tread;
What wilder Beast is harnessed yet to be,
Why, Brothers, wait, for you may live to see.

Our Politics are changing too,
For why should they stand still?
Our Demagogues must something do
The Offices to fill;
To save the State, they often change their mind,
To no opinion slavishly confined.

Our simple, antiquated sires
Got up a great parade,
About a certain whim of theirs,
That men were equal made,
And all entitled to be free beside;
And none but Tories did their whim deride.

But greater men have lived and died
Since those men passed away,
And proved it clearly that they lied,—
Aye, proved it clear as day,
That men, since Adam, are not made at all,
But now as *Babes* they first begin to squall.

And, not content to clench the Truth
By such an argument,
They prove, (and green the Saxon youth
Declining his assent,)
That colored men are *darker* than the whites,
And cannot claim equality of Rights.

Our Union often has been saved,
When on the very brink,
Though Abolitionists have raved
To break the golden link;
And men begin to entertain the hope
That it has still an inch or two of rope.

As Haman could not be content
While Mordecai was there,
Sitting so proud and insolent
With such a haughty air;
So Politicians glory all in vain,
While tempting Cuba still adheres to Spain.

We 've none of us been President,
Though some have near him been,—
I trust no Brother to that high ascent
Will e'er be *crawling* seen;
Of a mere Party never be the head,
A tool to deal to Demagogues their bread.

Should Senate walls become your home
For twice six years or so,
Don't let your childish passions foam,
Nor let your manners go,
But keep a steady hand upon the helm,
With graceful dignity your foes o'erwhelm.

The College is a little State,
A truthful miniature,
And often Faculties the weight
Of Cabinets endure;
For boys, like men, will revolutionize,
And put to straits the wisdom of the wise.

They have a sort of politics,
The canvass oft is warm,
Each bravely to his party sticks,
While angry grows the storm;
King Caucus holds his hard, despotic sway,
And sleepless nights precede election day.

Of one election I will sing,
Which tried the bravest soul:
I seem to hear the armor ring,
I list the drum-beat's roll;
O, long the fearful conflict raged,
And all our thoughts and all our hearts engaged.

Excited circles gather hot
Around each doubtful hearth,
Where ne'er before had been a thought
How much a vote is worth;
The humble finds his own importance grow,
As from the proud such kind attentions flow.

One's face is wreathed in blandest smiles,
Another's wears a frown,
One's features glow with cunning wiles,
Another studies brown;
While timid, anxious, modest candidates
Alternate fears depress and hope elates.

And when the balloting began
Grave questions oft arose,
As murmurs through the assembly ran
So near we came to blows,
That prudent ones were humbled by their fears
That Congress ruffians soon would find their peers.

'T is late, and dimly shine the lamps,
Neglected in the fray,
In fury wild the foeman stamps,
And burns to fight his way;
The night is dark, nor will the sullen sky
Allow one star through rifted clouds to pry.

Our Chairman sees the tempest swell,
As cool and unconcerned
As any deep and crystal well
By strongest iron curbed;
"Let's put him out," a stalwart champion cries
As passage through the crowd he rushing tries.

But hark! as through the opening door
  A well-known figure glides;
As strikes his cane upon the floor,
  How quick the storm subsides!
"I order you, as riotous young men,
Disperse instanter!" shouts Professor Ben.

Were we to craven cowards turned?
  Were we by fear dispersed?
Oh no, we gracefully adjourned,
  By Love not Fear coerced.
That voice, for us with wondrous power endued,
Would then a rougher tempest have subdued.

When storms have all their fury spent,
  And hushed the howling wind,
Not always are the clouds content,
  But linger still behind;
As if unwilling that the stars should see,
Or quite uncertain what the end may be.

A dreary silence, dark and deep,
  Succeeded that night-storm;
We knew not but its dismal sweep
  Might kindle new alarm.
While doubts were in our anxious minds revolved,
Without a threat, the Union was dissolved.

This done, the gloomy cloud retires,
  Spanned with the brightest bow,
Though rival zeal our souls inspires,
  Our hearts together flow:
And since, like Brothers here we yearly meet,
The white and blue entwined in union sweet.

These simple badges both are dear;
  We own their gentle thrall,
And yet forgive, if very near,
  And that before you all,
Though White may have the strongest spell for you,
Nearest my heart bind *I* the dear old Blue.

How many scenes rise fresh to view,
Of olden College days,
Of wicked scrapes just crawled through,
Which set the Town ablaze:
How sheep were pastured 'neath the College dome,
And Sages like observed the planets roam.

'T is said their tracks were plainly seen
Upon the lightning-rod,
Nor did our Swan an insult mean
When, with a gracious nod,
He told the wrathful shepherd how they came
To be in such an elevated frame.

How vagrant cows, with ghostly sheet,
The last the poor chum had,
Went bellowing through the village street
As if already mad;
No wonder, when that antiquated pail
Was dangling from her persecuted tail.

Of foot-balls running gauntlet rough,
Amid a host of foes,
Which proved at least whose shins were tough,
And who had tender toes;
Ah, dark his face who seized that harmless ball
And bore it to the recitation hall.

Of sorrow borne, and tears that fell,
When that old house was burned,
That bound the Common by a spell,
Before to Park it turned;
Though of such partners honestly afraid,
The flames, disgusted, seemed to crave our aid.

From tangled wood and river bank
We brought the budding trees,
And though you know not whom to thank,
We whisper, if you please,
That that old Common owes a lasting debt,
To the largest class that ever trod it yet.

Fashion has had its changes too,
  To very slight extent;
Perhaps a hundred times or so,
  Since Chandler, all intent
To save his shoes, yet guard against offense,
The lesson finished, hid them 'neath the fence.

Some fair ones think they ought to wear—
  I shall not mention what,—
For men of them most jealous are,
  And think they 're in a plot
To wrest our rightful sceptre from us too,
And seem to reign, as actually they do.

And men are growing feminine,
  Except about the face,
And he who shows the fairest skin
  Is noblest of his race;
The softest shawls begin to hug their necks,
And jewels sparkle on the sterner sex.

The eye is pleased to linger,
Not much disposed to roam,
Upon a lily finger
Where jewels seem at home;
If men will wear them, why, let me propose
That they shall let them dangle from the nose.

And when our elder Brothers here
Were young, their sisters plied
The busy wheel, without a tear;
If caught, no wounded pride
Mantled their dimpled cheeks with blushes o'er,
The rose's banner floated there before.

But now the damsels are at school,
And shame their Brothers oft,
Although they cannot wind a spool,
In learning soar aloft;
When fifty years again have rolled around,
Sisters Alumni with us may be found.

Accursed be the selfish boor
  Who 'd clog our sister's wings,
And tie her to the kitchen door,
  Or bind with leading strings
Her gentle genius plumed for loftiest flights,
No matter what are her disputed rights.

In olden times the Fathers learned
  To read, to spell, to write,
The quill its graceful figures turned;
  But since, such silly sight
Is rarely seen,—we scribble now, with gold or steel,
Such writing as would make the Fathers reel.

The Teachers whom they dearly loved,—
  They are not here to greet them,—
Some have to other fields removed,
  And some can never meet them;
For Death has called them to its sweet repose,
Life's labors ended, with its joys and woes.

The Younger find there linger still
The same familiar faces,
And Brothers now with honor fill
Some dear old Teachers' places;
The heads that once with raven locks were crowned
Are now with silver almond blossoms bound.

The Temple at whose sacred shrine
Our elder Brothers bowed,
Whose young affections loved to twine
Around its portals proud,
Has long since fed the fierce and cruel flames,
Nor can they find where they had carved their names.

But some things, Brothers, little change:
That silver Lake is all the same,
And yonder lofty mountain range
Unaltered since the white man came
And shared its solitude
With Indian rude.

The sky displays as bright a blue
As smiled upon the forest green,
And just such stars did e'er bestrew
That bending arch, as now are seen
In clusters sown,
Or all alone
In gentle radiance glowing,
Their limpid light forever flowing.

And Truth, though old,
Grows never gray;
The Ages fold
The young to-day
With unresisted arms,
But lend no brighter charms
To that which perfect came from Old Eternity,
And never while Jehovah is can changed be.

And now, before my timid muse,
O'ertasked, shall cease to sing,

I know you cannot but excuse,
Should I a tribute bring
To one whose name will thrill the coldest heart,
Perhaps will cause th' unbidden tear to start.

O would that I could now employ
Some Angel's tongue,
Whose fitting song
Might fill your hearts with purest joy;
For he could tell where in the sky
That Star's sweet light,
Though tranquil, bright,
Is shining in its sphere so high.

I.

Vermont, thy mountain breezes erst have fanned
The brow of warrior bold, of statesman sage,
And yet the Poet's mystic, waving wand
Will charm to life thy bright historic page:

Ah, such will live, the good, the great, the brave,
  Will live in grateful hearts, if not in song,—
Their hallowed deeds will never find a grave,
  Although unsung their fame may slumber long;
But *should* our honored great forgotten lie,
  Their names and mouldering dust together sleep,
Methinks our MARSH will be the last to die,
  The last to sink beneath Oblivion's deep,—
So many living words he left behind,
So many hearts his image have enshrined.

II.

We fear to lisp thy virtues, lest the flowers
  Around thy grave with blushes should reprove
The man whose crude, untried and humble powers
  Should rudely dare such sacred theme approach;
But then we love thee so, our burning heart
  So sweetly whispers to itself of thee,
It fain would try Divine Apollo's art,
  And, singing, set its silent music free.

Could I the pencil's magic power employ,
  I'd paint Philosopher, with lofty mien,
Accounting it his highest, purest joy
  To sit at JESUS' feet, and there be seen,
With holy, tranquil aspect, seizing all
The words that from the greatest Teacher fall.

III.

His Life was like a River, clear and deep,
  And calmly gliding toward its Ocean home;
No noisy tumult, rush, or maddened leap,
  Dashing the peaceful waters into foam;
The soul of Truth revealed herself to him,
  Disrobed of all fantastic, gaudy show,
Her Angel form, to most so dark and dim,
  Shone clearly forth with ever bright'ning glow;
We loved to look upon his noble mien,
  Capacious forehead, shading deep-set eyes,
That looked serene, as if they oft had seen,
  In realms of Beauty, heavenly visions rise;

A holy calm was ever on his face,
Tinged with a smile of sweet, peculiar grace.

IV.

As we recall his body, pale and worn,
  Trembling, as the harp trembles when its strings
Awaken deepest melodies,—we mourn
  That God so feebly guarded life's deep springs.
That modest tenement was far too frail
  For such a soul as his to dwell in long;
Such never-tiring thought could scarcely fail
  To do the strongest frame a fatal wrong.
  But God did chasten sore our selfish hearts,
That would have fettered to our chilly shore
A heart so pure,—a spirit fit to soar
  To brightest realms, whose sunlight ne'er departs,
Or lets the darkness in to furnish needless rest
For those who dwell forever with the Blest.

V.

Tremulous his voice,—with Truth 't was freighted so,
It wavered like an undulating strain
Of music, or like limpid rays that flow
From stars reflected trembling from the rippled main.
His manners bore an unaffected grace;
Enough for him to seem just what he was;
He loved us all, we saw it in his face,
And there we read our most effective laws.
He seemed to die—his form is shrouded now,
And hidden from our view—but there he sleeps;
And though we cannot see his pale, high brow,
Nor check the grief that, unresisted, creeps
Among our joys—that spot, so justly dear,
We 'll visit oft, and o'er it drop a tear.

But, Brothers, I have wearied you,—
To this fond hour I cling;
Of all this crowd, alas! how few
Will hear another sing

5*

When fifty years again shall roll away,
And there shall come like this another day!

Ere then the most of us will sleep
The sleep no waking knows,
For some there will be few to weep
When our poor eyelids close;
While others still shall slumber with the great,
When they shall lay aside the robes of state.

And some may find no other grave
Than such as strangers make,
When kindly from the drifting wave
They floating corses take;
While others' monuments shall proudly tell
The passing stranger where they bravely fell.

Whoever lives to see that day,
Will feel the same strange thrill,

Of which our Elder Brothers may
Soon tell us, if they will.
Of all this living multitude, who dare
Indulge the faintest hope of being there?

Brothers, where'er our footsteps roam,
When'er our pathways meet,
Though distant from our old sweet Home,
In fellowship complete,
Let U. V. M. sufficient pass-word be
To waken, ever, deepest sympathy!

WASHINGTON AND HIS MOTHER.

A POEM,

DELIVERED IN GRAND ISLE, FEBRUARY 22, 1855.

POEM.

I.

How blest was She, whose throbbing bosom bore
The lovely Babe, whom millions now adore!
How sweet to carry in her willing arms
The Sinless Child, adorned with all the charms
That Human Beauty, Purity Divine,
Could in the fairest, brightest Form combine.
How blest the pillow where His cheek
Did oft its little dimpled slumbers seek.
And this was Mary's lot, her priceless dower,—
O'ershadowed by the Spirit's Holy Power,
She gave the world the purest, noblest One,

Of Hope the Star, of Righteousness the Sun.
His childhood, youth, and early manhood, too,
Were hers—His life her joy, His death her wo.

II.

Many a mother, since, has borne a son,
Who has a race of brightest glory run;
Many an infant, doubtless, nestles now,
In gentle arms, upon whose lily brow,
There shines a star of Promise, all unseen
Except by Him, from whom no mortal screen
Can hide the Future's Promise or its Threat;
Who knows what is, nor can the Past forget.
Ah, fondly dreams the mother's hopeful heart,
The plaything now of Love's beguiling art;
And yet she cannot see the dazzling path
Of future glory, nor descry the wrath,
That brightens it,—'t is well, too fondly might
She crush, or speed too soon the birdlet's flight.

III.

No wonder that the favored Virgin's name,
Whose lot so blest, secured undying fame,
Should oft be chosen to adorn the child,
Around whose fragile form, yet undefiled,
Affection weaves so sweet, so strong a cord,
And names her from the mother of our Lord,
Disclosing, thus, the pleasant homage paid
To Mary, Heaven's chosen, honored Maid.
How can a mother fond more fitly tell
The Loves and Hopes that in her bosom swell?
What sweeter word can charm the maiden's ear,
Or lull the fount whence springs the pearly tear,
If kindly spoken, when the heart is glad,
Or softly whispered, when the heart is sad?

IV.

What countless multitudes this name have borne,
Yet 't is as sweet as if it ne'er was worn,—
'T will bear repeating till the end of time,

And sparkle even in the dullest rhyme;
To Mother, Sister, or to One more near,
Addressed, it bears a music ever dear.
It sounds so sweetly in the mother's song,
It flows so easy from the father's tongue,
So softly from the loving brother slips,
Tastes so like Nectar to the lover's lips—
If still unnamed, thy baby-wonder lies,
And each the sweetest word yet vainly tries
To find, sore plagued to name the budding Life,
Just whisper Mary, and you end the strife.

V.

'T is not because the Jewish maiden wore
The purest diadem e'er worn before,
Though Popes and pious Councils do declare
That Mary never sinned, I find nowhere
The evidence that she was wholly free
From poisoned sap, that flowed from that old Tree,
Whence all, but One, have drawn the fatal stain,

Of which we all so bitterly complain.
O no, the accents of the word are sweet—
If anything were needful to complete
Its charm, enough that She by it was known,
The mother of our Lord, and that alone
Would give the word a dear, magnetic spell,
Make deepest music in its letters dwell.

VI.

Of all the Marys that have lately bloomed,
Or have, as yet, been in our Land entombed,
This evening points us to the dearest One;
We can but love Her, for we love her Son,
If she was but a common woman, e'en,
Her fragrant laurels would be evergreen;
What higher fame, by woman could be won,
Than to be Mother of our Washington?
And yet this Mary's memory may be crowned
With all the virtues that are ever found;
Her station was a Mother's, nobly filled,

In all a Mother's wisdom deeply skilled,
Her mind so clear, her heart so deep and pure,
Bravely a Mother's care did she endure.

VII.

No Painter ever caught her winning grace,
Or limned the pleasing grandeur of her face,
She sought no Artist's aid to steal from Death
The transient tribute due his icy breath.
Her life to her seemed humble, and her work
A common task, but never did she shirk
The pleasant toil, or in the path of duty pause,
To seek display, or gain the world's applause.
No need of Painter's skill or Sculptor's art,
For her who wisely acts the Mother's part:
She paints herself upon the plastic mould,
Her child will e'er her truest likeness hold;
The Father thus the crumbling stone outlives,
The fading canvas fainter memory gives.

VIII.

If, then, our Country's Mary we would see,
O, Image bright, our eyes must gaze on Thee!
Thy lofty frame, thy grand, majestic mein,
Wherein all manly virtues may be seen,
Reveals the likeness of that rev'rend One
Who gave the world our Washington.
Her truth and goodness mirrored in thy face,
Her honest frankness, dignity and grace;
Nor need we make a toilsome pilgrimage,
To find the picture of the Hero, Sage:
'T is everywhere, in every humble home,
As well as 'neath the Capitol's high dome,—
We need no guide to tell us where to look,
In gilded Palace, or in Cottage nook.

IX.

The child as well would need the stranger's aid
To tell the likeness, if with other's laid,
Of his own Father,—dim indeed the eyes

That fail at once that face to recognize:
If chiselled with a Powers's wondrous skill,
Or rudely whittled, lo! we know it still,—
If painted by an Allston's magic wand,
Or coarsely graven by a Tyro's hand.
Methinks that modern Artist, called the Sun,
Would even smile to paint our Washington,
For greater work by him has ne'er been done,
Since this new business was by him begun.
If e'er a mortal could endure his rays,
'T was He could calmly meet his burning gaze.

X.

It was in seventeen hundred thirty-two,
A hundred three and twenty years ago
This night, in olden mansion, first was heard,
A feeble infant's cry, and first there stirred
The little throbbing heart, ere long to bear
A nation's burden, and to bravely dare
A monarch's ire, and guide the raging crest

Of waves up-swelling from a nation's breast.
The interest in that Babe was just the same
As that which parents always feel,—for fame
Had sent to them no premonitions bright,
No angel's vision blessed the mother's sight;
The tender gazing of that happy eye
Revealed no consciousness of glory nigh.

XI.

She sung to him the mother's lullaby,
Nor dreamed that she was nursing Liberty;
She rocked him, just as other mothers do,
Nor dreamed she rocked a Young Republic too;
In those soft eyes, whose mildly radiant gleam,
Stole sweetly through the loving mother's dream,
She saw no martial ardor brightly burn,
No flower seems gentler, in enamelled urn.
The dimpled hand, that grasped her shining pearls,
That pressed her bosom, or deranged her curls,
Gave little promise e'er to wield the sword,

His tiny lips to give the chieftain's word,—
Though gemmed with stars, the Heaven's unclouded
blue
Conceals what lies beyond a mortal's view.

XII.

She meant to train him, in her humble way,
To do good service in his coming day;
She thought the surest way to make him great
Would be to make him good, and, patient, wait,
For Virtue's own reward, the richest store
That man can gather;—and still more,
To make him wise, to cultivate his mind,
His mind and heart in harmony combined.
And afterward, 't is said, when tidings came
Of his great victory, the modest dame
Looked up, betraying not the least surprise,
A mother's triumph only in her eyes;
She wondered not, though rapturous her joy,
She said, "For George was always a good boy."

XIII.

Good boys will make good men, and women, too,
Good girls will be,—the tree will ever grow
Just as the twig is bent, the Poets say,
As tranquil evening crowns the peaceful day;
So thought our matron, and she lived to see
The graceful twig become the lofty tree;
She traced no windings in its comely growth,
Straight upward soared his youth and manhood both.
Although to human eyes that infant's lot unseen,
Another looked the mystic leaves between;
Beside the earthly, there were angels there,
Bestowing on the helpless one unsleeping care,
Of childhood ever guarded they the rest,
In manhood, mailed his oft imperilled breast.

XIV.

As wise in council as in battle brave,
He meant to win, or find a soldier's grave;
Although he might his brow with stars bestud,

He would not rashly waste a brother's blood,
For him no victor's laurels seemed to be
Deserved, save such as made his country free.
No foeman's malice ever nerved his arm,
He sought to do no human being harm.
He loved his men, and tried to save their lives,
He knew they left at home their children, wives;
Nor did he wish his enemies to slay,
Unless they put them madly in his way;
He had no relish for the bloody strife,
His cause was just, to that he pledged his life.

XV.

O, there were days of darkness and of gloom,
When Freedom seemed enshrouded for the tomb;
When stoutest hearts, so weary and forlorn,
Began the future's misery to mourn;
They had provoked a proud and haughty realm,
A cruel monarch scowled fiercely at the helm.
Their righteous cause seemed ready to be crushed,

The voice of Hope to be forever hushed.
Suppose a Washington had faltered then,
And left uncheered his sad, despairing men;
Suppose an Arnold had our chieftain been,
And his base eyes the threatening cloud had seen;
Alas! our souls from such a vision shrink,
Our hearts to such a depth of horror sink.

XVI.

Our Hero stood and eyed the gathering storm,
And higher towered his firm, unbending form,
His hand, untrembling, grasped the trusty blade,
He called on God his country's cause to aid;
His soldiers caught his calm and holy trust,
And trod their guilty terrors in the dust;
They saw the pledge of triumph in his eye,
They vowed to gain it, or with him to die.
Through all the perils of those changeful years,
He wavered never with the nation's fears;
Such wisdom with such courage was combined,

To noble aims his purpose so confined,
The Records of the Past you search in vain,
You find none *like* him to reward your pain.

XVII.

The foeman felt the strange, mysterious spell,
Securely guarding life's brave citadel,
He could not take untrembling, steady aim
Toward that majestic, angel-guarded frame;
The Red Man's arm was weak when he was near,
The Briton felt a new, peculiar fear;
The death-hail fell in showers around his path,
Yet ever harmless spent its potent wrath.
If ever Heaven raised a mortal man,
To carry out some great, predestined plan,
But few can doubt that Washington was sent,
And formed to execute some high intent;
He had such fitness for his sacred task,
He seemed an angel, in a human mask.

XVIII.

When war had ceased, and they who sternly braved
In perils, proudly Freedom's Banner waved,
O, who but he could take the nation's helm,
And safely guide the new created Realm?
Although his spirit, sweet retirement sought,
Where unambitious virtues might be wrought,
The New Republic then was yet too weak
To suffer him such quiet bliss to seek.
If as a soldier, he so brave and wise,
That brighter stars have ne'er adorned the skies,
His courage and his wisdom failed him not,
When Peace new trophies to his honor brought,
Ambition's proffers met his proud disdain,
He left the chair of State without a stain.

XIX.

Our country's youthful history may boast
Of mighty men, a strangely brilliant host,
But Washington alone pre-eminent,

Demands the homage of a Continent;
Ah yes, the *world* will love to gaze on him,
When Heavenly Peace shall War's red glory dim;
Though other men the noblest deeds have done,
In him their virtues all combine in One.
And now, when partizans their leaders praise,
And seek their names to highest honor raise,
When other language fails their idle tongue,
To cap the climax of their fulsom song,
With mighty leap from where they first begun,
They say, "he is another Washington."

XX.

Some foolish men, provoked by zeal profane,
Will soar still higher, ne'er to light again,—
For such, inflated with so thin a gas,
Unless some dire explosion comes to pass,
Can ne'er descend to solid earth and tread
Where common sense to common truth is wed,
As if they had wherewith his merits could be weighed!

As if another such had e'er been made.
No doubt, in Learning men are more profound,
And Learning oft with Folly may be found,
In Eloquence there are who may excel,
Who 'd fail to weave their words with deeds so well,
And men as valiant tread the battle field,
Who must to Him the palm of wisdom yield.

XXI.

From other men he stands so far "apart,"
So "grand, peculiar," to the Freeman's heart,
That there is room for many a smaller star,
To whirl within his sphere, yet beam afar
From Him, so far indeed they nothing lose;
With him in competition none would choose
To bring their brightness, but contented glow,
With lesser lights, that shine in spheres below.
Bend not the knee before the gorgeous Sun,
It would be wrong to *worship* Washington,—
Yet may the dismal morning never dawn

When highest rev'rence shall for him be gone,
Whene'er Americans shall *lightly* speak
His name,—make haste, a grave for Freedom seek!

XXII.

He died too soon,—ah no, God called for him,
Before his strength decayed, or eye was dim;
No second childhood claims our sympathy,
No long imprisonment e'er he was free:
He fell while garlands wreathed his honored brow,
As proudest Oaks before the tempest bow,
With all their blooming foliage richly spread,
To ease their fall and make their dying bed;
He passed away before his heart had bled,
To see Oppression triumph o'er the dead,
Ere men had dared those Doctrines to deride,
For which his Brothers fought, for which they died;
He slept ere Slavery had been found to be
The chosen Bridegroom of fair Liberty!

XXIII.

'T is passing pleasant, in these *honest* days,
When *some* men relish still the Hero's praise,
To think how kindly, yet how plainly spoke
Our Chieftain, e'er the golden bowl had broke;
No bitter taunts were hurled, no rude reproof,
His pale lips pleaded in the slave's behoof,
Before the solemn majesty of Death,
While all the Nation, listening, held its breath:
All men should have their rightful liberty,
All men are equal, is high Heaven's decree;
We did not fight to rivet human chains,
'T is not for this our blood-bought Freedom reigns;
My slaves are free, I leave no bonds behind,
Ho, Brothers, see, I every cord unbind.

XXIV.

Near Vernon's Mount the Patriot Father sleeps,
And o'er his ashes Heaven nightly weeps.

Many a pious pilgrim hieth here,
To pay the transient tribute of a tear.
It seemeth holy, near the humble mound,
And hushed the footfall's hesitating sound,
A mighty Presence seems to fill the air,
With muffled steps the stranger walketh there.
No other grave has such mysterious power
To awe the soul. Far distant be the hour
When thoughtless men shall break its sweet repose!
O never while Potomac's water flows!
Aye, let him sleep where his last work was done,
In holy slumbers rest, our WASHINGTON!

OYSTER-SUPPER MEDLEY.

MEDLEY.

THERE is a little word I hate to speak,
When bearded men some trivial favor seek,
But when the Ladies ask, how can I say,
In view of all their gentle kindness, nay?
With aching brow, with worn and weary hands,
They cheerful toil, to meet this eve's demands,—
Can I refuse my jaded brain to task,
When only, my poor simple rhymes they ask?

But what shall be my theme, ye gracious ones?
The muffled brook, in winter, silent runs:
The soothing murmur of the silver waves,

Still as the lips of loved ones in their graves,
Is hushed beneath the solid crystal shield,
To which the fiercest tempest has to yield.
There is no sighing now among the trees,
No leaves to dally with the loving breeze;
The frost-defying evergreens, oppressed
With snows that drift upon the mountain's breast,
Refuse to heave the melancholy sigh,
Unto the wailing wind that rushes by;
The warbling birds have gone to fairer climes,—
Where shall I get the music for my rhymes?

That little fellow, even, that persists
In calling Phœbe often as he lists,
Whether because she never is at home,
Or never ready at his call to come,—
Like fussy wives, who try their husbands so,
When oft reminded that 't is time to go,—
Or whether really he thinks her name
The sweetest one that ever fann'd the flame

Of love, within a throbbing, feathered breast,
And therefore sings it with such tireless zest,
And loves upon the darling word to dwell,
I think 't would take a Daniel e'en to tell.

But he has gone, and Phœbe with him, too,
Where flowers bloom, their balmy breath to woo,
And also that mysterious little sprite,
Whose malice, or some selfish spite,
Keeps telling us that Katy did, and yet
Won't tell us what, to keep us in a fret,
Has left us in a most perplexing maze
Of dire suspicions as to Katy's ways.
In vain we try to read those laughing eyes,
Or chase the roguish smile that, rippling, flies
Around her secret's mute but rosy seal,
That could, but will not, break at our appeal.
Come, Katy, tell us now what you have done,
And spoil that tattler's tantalizing fun.

One of the songsters of the summer time,
Now gone to Carolina's sunny clime,
I always greeted with a thrill of joy,
Whose praise shall now my rustic harp employ.

I love to hear the Robin sing,
The Lark, when warbling on the wing,
The Chickadee's sweet matin lays,
The Oriole, of golden rays,
The Ground-Bird's clear and silvery notes,
The Swallow, twittering as he floats,—
But yet, of all the choir, I think,
The sweetest far, the Bobolink.

Happy to gain his Northern home,
In fragrant June, he loves to come,
And seeks the meadow, green and bright,
Where berries greet his gladdened sight:
Now poised upon a spire of grass,
As pert and merry as a lass,—

Now perched upon the homely fence,
As if of little consequence,
If he can only sit and sing,
And 'round his merry carols fling,—
Then floating off upon the air,
He sprinkles music everywhere:
It bubbles from his plumpy breast,
Now on the wing, and now at rest,
He hardly stops for taking breath,
And almost sings himself to death.
To vie with him they well might shrink
Who would keep time with Bobolink.

He does not like the leafy groves,
Where others hide to chant their loves,
Nor does he seek the shady tree,
Where timid warblers love to be.
The green below, above the blue,
He loves to quaff the fragrant dew,
In brilliant sunshine likes to swim,

While bubbles out his grateful hymn.
Nor does he vainly soar too high,
As if he wished to reach the sky,
But skims along the clover heads,
Where lurk the tempting berry beds.
Obedient to a loving will,
His joyous nature fears no ill;
He acts as if he knew us all,
And would be glad to make a call,
If there was room for him to sing,
And keep the sunshine on his wing.
As well forbid the spring to play,
The gushing fountain's silver spray,
The rill to leap its rocky brink,
As hush the jolly Bobolink.

The careless boys delight to try
Their skill, and let their missiles fly,
But off he floats, without offence,
And music gives as recompense.

To others drown he seems to strive,
And every feather seems alive;
At once he flies, and laughs, and sings,
And showers music from his wings,
And looks so waggish in his eye,
Toward th' enraptured passer-by,
He can but smile to see him blink,
And cry, "Here goes the Bobolink!"

Perhaps he may be deemed too bold,
Not shaped in very modest mould,
But then I like his "I don't care!"
He says it with so sweet an air.
His bosom is so full of joy,
His crowded throat he must employ,
Without a thought of how it seems
To pour out music in such streams.
Ye prudish dames, and maids demure,
And solemn men, so gravely pure,
Do not despise our little friend,

Whose child-like ways you cannot mend,—
I would that you such bliss could drink,
And warble like the Bobolink.

Apace will come the sober hours,
Ere long will fade the early flowers,
We may in darkness soon repose,
Or hide in silence voiceless woes ;
Let gladness wing us up the Hill,
Then downward let us warble still.
Until in gloom compelled to sink,
Welcome the fun-full Bobolink.

And this reminds me of a dream I had,
About this jolly little feathered lad.
After a weary, musing, homesick stroll,
I thought I lay upon a mossy knoll,
That gayly smiled beneath a tropic sky,
And watched the birds that floated silent by.

A waving rice-field spread its treasures there,
To tempt the winged rovers of the air,
I saw a bird arrest his weary flight,
And on a rice-head poise his body light,
As I had seen him, on the bending spire
Of grass, where Phœbus feeds a milder fire.
How changed! his gaudy plumage turned to gray,
And he was silent through the livelong day.
I knew him by the twinkle of his eye,
I thought of home, and heaved a bitter sigh.
He seemed to know me, and essayed to sing,
My presence seemed a memory to bring
Of other skies, of summer berries red,
That lay so fragrant in their Northern bed.

What ails thee, little friend, at length said I,
Why do you all in dreary silence fly?
Give me a song like that I used to hear,
So full of rapture and so full of cheer.

Alas, I cannot sing!
I left my heart, and could not bring
My music with me, to this land of slaves,
Where cheerless toilers hurry to their dismal graves.

These rice-fields, could they tell,
The fearful tales they know so well,
Would burden all the air with such a wail,
The stoutest heart would quake, the fiercest spirit quail.

This damp and poisoned air
Has carried many a captive's prayer,
For vengeance on the trader,—who has riven
So many loving hearts,—and wafted it to Heaven.

I 've heard him as he toiled,
Cursing the Tyrant, who had spoiled
His olden home,—have seen his sturdy frame
Quiver with anguish, when he sighed some loved one's name.

I 've seen a Mother quake,
As if her very heart would break,
And clasp her hands upon her aching breast,
Where once her little babe was oft so fondly pressed.

It was but yesterday,
I saw a happy boy at play
Upon that very knoll where you are now,
And sorrow had not tinged his smooth and sunny brow.

His mother wore a smile,
Letting her little one beguile,
With transient joy, her fears that seldom slept,
And then, as if she sinned, she clasped her boy and wept.

He caught the burning tear
Upon his dimpled cheek, while clear
And loud his bird-like notes came gushing out,
And put her wakened terrors to a speedy rout.

Just then a monster came,
Who even bore a Christian's name,
And features of a Human face, though dim,
And bade the frightened boy to rise and follow him.

"For you are mine," said he.
"Nay, God has given the child to me,"
The wretched mother cried, while 'round her twin'd
The soft, round arms, the heartless Trader would unwind.

And, Oh! the fearful shriek,
When cheek was pressed to scalded cheek,
That wailing cry of agony so sore,
When, torn apart, away the struggling child they bore.

The little outstretched hands,
The pleading looks, the stern commands,
The last, wild, mingled glance, that flashed amid
The blinding flood,—the crushed, defenceless, falling dead!

In yonder burial place,
Where many of the friendless race
Are lying, is the murdered mother's tomb:
Her boy is weeping in a distant stranger's home.

How can you wonder, Friend,
That I can never, never blend
My happy notes with curses, groans and sighs,
That morning, noon, and e'en at silent midnight, rise?

Sad Wanderer, return,
And drink from Freedom's crystal urn.
Summer will soon resume her joyous reign,
When I will hie me where we all may sing again.

What think you, Friends, of such a dismal dream?
A fit of indigestion does it seem?
Or is it all an Abolition whim,
That fills my soul with fancies grim?

Well, let the vision pass!
What steps are tripping o'er the glass?
They sound like Fairies out upon a train,—
Ah, they are snow-flakes tapping on the window pane.

What ails my shouting boy?
He 's crazy with some new-born joy.
The birds are mingling music with the snow,
Their song is sweet, but, list! how soft and low.

See them on the cherry-trees,
Heedless of the biting breeze,
Laughing as it rushes;
On the currant-bushes,
See them shake their wings,—
Heaven bless the little things!

Ah! not of earth, the snow-birds seem to me,
Their native realm with snow-flakes seems to be;
They float down with them from the bending sky,

Then melt away, or back to Heaven fly,
Or Spirits of another, better world,
Whose plains with dew, and not with frost impearl'd.

What notes are those that ring so clear,
So welcome to the listening ear?
O, 't is the joyous peal of bells,
That every kindling bosom swells.
A shaggy robe protects the form,
And keeps the sturdy driver warm,
While snugly nestles by his side,
Buried in furs, a happy Bride.
Not buried quite,—her head is bare,
Defying all the frosty air;
Only a veil, at least, is on it,
The keenest cannot see a bonnet.

O for the olden days, when girls
In downy hoods concealed their curls:
The hoods of purple, lined with roses,

Wherein the dimpled chin reposes,
Folded close, it softly presses
Cheeks that blush in its caresses,
Revealing only flashing eyes,
Or lips the Frost-King vainly tries
To chill with kisses as he flies,
And reddens to his sweet surprise.

Do you remember, Friends, those days,
When Eden blossomed in our sleighs,
As o'er the gleaming ice we flew,
And Heaven had so sweet a blue?
Or over banks we bounded so,
Glad to be buried in the snow,
Because we loved to lift the girls,
And see them shake their glittering curls,
Protesting that we did not know
How we could help that overthrow?

Ah! when will hoods return again,

The objects now of proud disdain?
The hoods of purple, lined with red,
'Round which, though summer bloom had fled,
There hovered such a magic spell,
The lads who felt it could not tell
Why any one should long for Spring;
As if her balmy breeze could fling
A sweeter fragrance from its wing,
Than floated from that pouting thing,—
The hood of purple, tipped with red,
Which modern lasses seem to dread.

But Fashion pleads a reason good,
For leaving off the purple hood,
For any one may learn at school,
That human heads should e'er be cool.
Indeed, the wire with ribbons on it,
Which people strangely call a bonnet,
Is quite too heavy and too hot
For such a well-protected spot;

And so the hair, that used to flow
In tresses on a neck of snow,
Or gathered in a lofty dome,
Surmounted by a shining comb,
In wavy fold, or cunning curl,
That set our hearts in such a whirl,
Regardless of the mother's tears,
Has yielded to the barber's shears.

Some years ago, Miss Bloomer thought
Fashion was in her logic caught;
But lo! the wily Princess fled,
With all her hooped trophies spread.
To dress like men, fie, what a shame!
Cried out the gay and saucy dame.
If one rejoins: Why shears employ,
To make your girl look like a boy?
How stupid! Fogies, don't you know
What lots of time a girl would throw
Away upon her aching head,

That should be spent in making bread!
And think of carrying such a load,
On Life's o'erloaded, slippery road:
Our heads, they must be cool and light,
That thought and feeling may be bright,
And if our Brothers hate to see
Their sisters from such burdens free,
Why, let them throw their razors, where
Some old disgusted grizzly bear
May tramp them out of sight and mind,
And lessons give to human kind.

Perhaps the partridge may be tamed;
Perhaps a rifle, wisely aimed,
May trim an errant comet's tail;
A miser hush an orphan's wail;
Perhaps a river may be coaxed
To start up hill, and not be hoaxed;
Perhaps, if you should sorely teaze,
Old Mansfield may be made to sneeze;

The politician may be tired
Of office, or, by wit inspired,
May lay his robes of honor by,
And let another fellow try
To guide the helm of state awhile,
Till he can make his yellow pile;
The grumbler may be made to laugh;
The toper pure cold water quaff,—
But never hope to see the day
When Fashion shall resign her sway!
Aye, if she bids us spread the sail,
No matter if it blows a gale,
We yield at once:—if 't is her mind
That we should trim it to the wind,
We take a reef, without delay,
And no uneasiness betray.
In vain we fret, in vain we scold,
We all obey, the young and old!
The Quaker, even, yields to Fate,
And narrows down his broad-brimmed hat;

Those model bonnets, long and clean,
Within whose satin folds were seen
Those pure, sweet faces, red and white,
Away beyond the saucy light,
Have shortened, and, we grieve to say,
Reveal to us but common clay.

The music of the human voice,
That makes our loving hearts rejoice,
Is clearest, sweetest, when the frost
Has frightened off the feathered host.
The Singing-School has countless charms,
To temper Winter's icy arms.
Who heeds his rude and chilly grasp,
Who reins and something else may clasp,
And gayly start the merry bells,
And bound along the snowy swells,
That lie across the drifted path,
The storm has piled up in his wrath?

The bright, glad faces gathered there,
The laughter peals that throng the air,
The shafts of wit, the repartee,
The silent feeling one may see,
Though words refuse the tale to tell,
Making the joyous bosom swell;
The sacred song, the social glee,—
How sweet the Singing-School may be!

And then the precious songs of Home!
O who, wherever he may roam,
Can e'er forget the simple lays
He learned in early childhood days?
The Father leads the loving choir,
Gathered around the crackling fire;
Along the wave of graver notes,
A Mother's angel music floats,
And children's voices sweetly blend,—
O that such bliss might never end!

And Winter has such silences,
Amid the bare and leafless trees,
When e'en the hum of bees is still,
And snows have hushed the tinkling rill.

Amid the wilderness of Polar snow and ice,
A Traveller stood beneath the dim Auroral light,—
No singing brook, or whispering tree, nor sighing leaf,
To break the stern and gloomy silence of the night.

He oft had seen the ocean in its roughest mood,
Beheld the tropic sky, when fearful tempests raged,
Surveyed the battle-field, when howled the fiends of
War,
Grim multitudes in wild and bloody strife engaged.

But yet of all the memories the Hero held,
Of fearful scenes, that filled his soul with awe profound,
None could surpass the breathless stillness of the night,
The depth of silence brooding o'er the Arctic ground.

The Night is sometimes awful in our genial clime,
When silent stars are floating o'er their field of blue,
And all the breezes sleep, and heart-throbs sound so
loud,
And we can hear the blood our veins careering through.

But even then the murmuring of distant waves,
The winds have lashed through all the day, is heard,
Like the soft moanings of the chastened child that sleeps,
And yet reveals how deep the fountain has been stirr'd.

Perhaps some solitary Owl the silence breaks,
Or wakeful Whippoorwill may start its echoes shrill,
Or if no living voice is found to break the spell,
We hear the ceaseless murmur of the sleepless rill.

The house of Death is awful, when the loved have
wept,
And sobbed themselves asleep, and watchers slowly
tread,

Their breathing half-suppressed, with soft and muffled feet,
As if afraid the lightest step would wake the dead.

The Grave-Yard is an awful place, with its still stones,
And wavy mounds, beneath which lie the garner'd dead,
Where willows nightly gather tears, to shed at dawn,
When sunlight wakes the breeze, and pearls the grassy bed.

But, O! the Soul is awful, when, withdrawing from the world,
We seek its inner chambers, filled with shadowy light,
Alone with our own Spirit, something may be felt
More fearful than the silence of an Arctic night!

That sacred breath of God, invisible, but felt,
In which our startled thoughts are floating silently,
Our Being's destiny revealed so dimly there,
So soon to be unfolded in Eternity.

MISCELLANEOUS.

FOR THE FOURTH OF JULY.

Let others sing of foreign lands,
  And hymn the praise of other climes,
Where rivers roll o'er golden sands,
  And bluer skies the mountain climbs:
Be mine the lot, with unpretending lays,
In humblest verse, to chant my Country's praise.

Let Bards heroic numbers roll,
  And tell of deeds of ancient fame,
With later Heroes fill the scroll,
  Crowned with the bravest warrior's name:
My muse would hover o'er old Plymouth Rock,
Where first was planted Freedom's fruitful stock.

O Robinson, thrice glorious thou,
Lingering there in banishment,
With Prayer to speed the Ocean plow,
With Angel Pilot all content:
No ship was ever manned by nobler men,
Than graced the goodly, fragrant May-Flower then.

Their names, a constellation bright
Of clustering jewels, gleaming fair,
As ever gemmed the brow of Night,—
Why should I choose a single star?
When grouped, their radiance shines in union sweet,
For equal fame, an equal song is meet.

But cold December is the time
For us of Pilgrim sires to sing;
The rushing blasts of Winter chime
Best with the memories that bring
Their perils, toils and sufferings to mind,
Best time a garland on their brows to bind.

The Summer's verdure, then, has fled,
And gone the flowers of Spring,
But evergreens we weave instead,
Away all fading emblems fling:
Memorials their deeds more lasting claim,
Than flowers' sweet but evanescent fame.

Of other times this day reminds,
Of other men it tells a tale:
A record bright of those unwinds,
Who launched on bloody seas their sail,
Who nailed their flag to Freedom's sturdy mast,
And pledged them each to leave that banner last.

O WASHINGTON! thou glorious One,
Standing apart from other men,
Like some great star, itself a sun,
No twinkling light, but pure serene:
So calmly beams thy simple majesty,
To worship thee were scarce idolatry.

And JEFFERSON, whose liberal soul
Demanded equal human rights,
Of Brotherhood the undivided whole,
Not merely for the favored Whites:
Thy realm so bright, is clear enough defined,
Whatever other stars with thee combined.

And ADAMS, HANCOCK, FRANKLIN, too,
Their radiant names bestud the sky,
While others gem the smiling blue,
And dimmest eyes their place descry;
And Heaven never blushes, when the tranquil night
Reveals her diadem, so gorgeous and so bright.

Of Freedom this the natal day,
A day of peril to our sires,
But Right they leaned on, as their stay,
And Heaven fanned the new-born fires:
To God they looked with brave but humble heart,
And nobly each performed his glorious part.

They bowed to God alone, as King,
To Him they thought the crown belonged,
Beneath the shelter of His wing,
Around their holy banner thronged:
Though weak themselves, they wielded Heaven's might,
And, risking all, they harnessed for the fight.

Though long and drear the bloody strife,
And often Hope lay down to die,
Our God restored her waning life,
And bade the lowering gloom to fly:
Through darkest clouds the Brave discovered light,
Though black beneath, the upper side was bright.

And when the Foe laid down his arms,
And bade our shores a glad adieu,
And Freedom showed her blood-bought charms
To our enraptured Fathers' view,
Flushed with their triumph, did they treacherous prove,
And leave their early for another love?

They loved her when they vainly sighed,
And on their galling fetters strained,
When forced her angel form to hide,
And all the world her charms disdained:
Nor did they fling their sacred pledge away,
When blushed the dawn of their victorious day.

Shall we, their sons, less faithful be,
To God, to Truth, to Freedom, less?
With wealth and power contented we,
And baser thoughts our souls possess?
If so, then let us ask our Sovereign King,
The blackest cloud o'er all His Heaven fling.

If so, let's seek the honored graves,
Where sleeps the dust of nobler men,
Their relics give the Ocean waves,
And bid them moan forever then:
For Human Freedom will have breathed her last,
Buried beneath the ruins of the Past.

In vain will other nations seek
  To raise aloft the battered flag,
The strong will triumph o'er the weak,
  And proudly will the banner drag,
Through seas of blood, and over desolated homes,
Where, now, with stealthy tread the Tyrant roams.

JOHN BROW

'Tis said, " Oppression makes the w

Such madness, BROWN, was thi

not brook

A wrong thyself, and others' sorro

Thou could'st not on thy outrag

With cold, unfeeling heart, nor patient wait,

Till God should break the Bondman's galling chain;

So brooding madly o'er his wretched fate,

You sought to rend his fetters, but in vain.

It may not be in vain, O Brother, brave!

Your wondrous daring has at least revealed

[illegible] may raise the turbid wave
[illegible]tion.—Slavery's doom is sealed!
[illegible] the fearful curse extend?
[illegible] hurry on its end?

[illegible] has raised thy scaffold high,
[illegible] wonted dignity,
[illegible] world to come and see thee die,
[illegible] crime—too great a love of Liberty!
[illegible] will see, and give their sympathy,
[illegible] the [illegible] crowd, whose shouts shall rise
[illegible] thy spirit, panting to be free,
[illegible] wafted to the pitying skies.
[illegible] Evil that has crazed thy soul,
The gazing millions load with curses loud,
And those who pray will never cease to roll
Of earnest prayers an ever-deepening cloud,
To Heaven, till God shall hear His chosen ones,
And break the bonds of Afric's bleeding sons.

'T were vain for us to chide thy rashness now,
  Or blame the zeal that bore thee to thy fate;
In tears, we weave a garland for thy brow,
  With aching heart, thy martyrdom we wait.
We know thy noble hands were tinged with blood,
  We feel the wrong that thou hast madly done,
Thy motive was to do thy Brothers good,—
  On nobler Purpose never looked the sun.
Thy scaffold is not far from Heaven's gate,
  And countless Angels will attend thee there,
Unseen of mortals, but with joy elate,
  Once more a Soul so great to sky-ward bear.
For rarely, in these basely selfish days,
Doth Earth for Heaven a genuine Hero raise.

NOTE.—I believe that I have no more right to go into a Slave State to meddle with any of its institutions, than I have to go to Cuba, Mexico, France, or Russia. Still, I cannot but admire the wondrous Christian Heroism displayed by JOHN BROWN. He fatally erred, but it was nevertheless on the side of the Right, and for the oppressed. God will bring good out of it.

AMOS LAWRENCE.

The tiny bud contains the coming flower,
  The twig the young tree's future form reveals;
As each is faithful in the trying hour,
  So each its undeveloped future seals.
The one may nourish in its fragrant core
  The fatal germ of premature decay;
To every breeze the other bending o'er,
  May grow unsightly in its wanton play.
Our LAWRENCE in his youth began to be
  The noble man he afterward became;
From vice and every evil habit free,
  His early virtues gained undying fame.
He bravely vanquished every youthful lust,
And early learned in God to trust.

With firm, elastic tread, he takes his place
  Upon the busy stage of active Life,
With eye undaunted, and with princely grace,
  He dons the armor, and he courts the strife;
Exacting of each moment as its flies,
  A golden tribute, Time is true to him,
And men confide in one so prompt and wise,
  Whose lustrous truth no tempting bribe can dim.
These Friends he early won, and never lost:
  Knowledge—of men, events, of Nature, God;
Industry—paying of thrift the honest cost;
  Honor—that ne'er in doubtful pathways trod;
Goodness—of vision large, and wealth of Heart;
With Piety—unmasked by gaudy Art.

God owned him, and from every side there flowed
  A stream to swell the tide of his success;
On trusty waves his vessel ever rode,
  And fiercest tempests wafted but to bless.

As rivers that confine themselves to Earth,
  Refusing tribute to the bounteous Sea,
Returning to the womb that gave them birth,—
  So seems the useless Miser's wealth to me.
Not such was his,—the streams came flowing in,
  To leave again, to bear, in countless rills,
Relief for sorrow, antidotes for sin,
  A healing balm for Life's resistless ills;
Smiles to rekindle in the orphan's face,
And joys to thrill the humblest of his race.

His bounty gladdened Childhood's merry dawn,
  And Age was brighter for his genial gifts;
The School has freely from his treasures drawn,
  A Monument its lofty summit lifts,—
A record, not of ancient deeds alone,
  Of those who bared their breasts to bloody foes,
For God and Liberty,—the chiselled stone
  Should tell, through whom the stately pile arose.
A steward, faithful to his sacred trust,

He understood why God had blessed him so;
He worshipped not his heaps of shining dust,
He worshipped God, and bade his riches go
On errands sweet of mercy, truth and love,
And laid his real treasures up above.

The Evening came, and with it sorrow too,
The furnace oft was hot, and he was tried;
But trials only seemed to sweetly woo
A balmier breath from Heaven, opening wide,
And wider still, its pearly gates, to let
The light and glory out in richer beams,
To gild the cloud in whose soft folds were met
Mercy and Truth, in sweetly blended gleams.
One like the Son of God e'er seemed to be
With him, in darkest hours of sorest grief,
And, conscious of that cheering Presence, he
Was ever happy with his lovely Chief.
To Life's last verge, he worked for God and Man,
And now of new-born stars he leads the van.

A life like his doth never, never die!
  Unearthed his spirit is,—Mount Auburn holds
His precious dust; but there, in yon sweet sky,
  A star is newly planted,—Heaven folds
The radiant One upon her bosom bright!
  No power can pluck from thence the beaming gem;
Long will it shine with steady, glowing light,
  To smile on Goodness, baseness to condemn.
Look up, O Youth! behold that gentle Star!
  Ye sordid ones, look up, and blush your shame!
Courage, ye noble Brave! there beams afar
  A glory bright, that dims all other fame,—
The glory of the Good Man's cherished worth,
In Heaven jewelled, and enshrined onEarth!

DR. BAILEY.

What wail is floating on the Ocean's breath,
   That thrills with anguish Freedom's broad domain?
Of whom bereft the world, insatiate Death!
   And added to thy ever-swelling train?
Hast thou an aged Warrior called to rest,
   Whose battles all were fought, and victories won?
Whose shield had fallen from his trembling breast,
   His helmet laid aside, his work all done?
   Oh, no,—thou hast our noblest Captain slain,
With all his armor on, when darkest night
Was fiercely struggling with the dawning light,
   His plume so proudly coursing o'er the plain.
Our land is rich in brave and noble men,
But will a BAILEY bless the world again?

His earnest words, though strong in Reason's might,
Were tempered ever with celestial light ;
The Press he wielded for a holy cause,
Obedient always to the sternest laws
Of frankness, truth and noble courtesy,
Undaunted and from vulgar shackles free,
Proclaiming boldly, to unwilling ears,
The thoughts that wake the guilty Tyrant's fears.
And yet his only purpose was to bless,
To swell the tide of human happiness ;
He loved his fellows, though he hated Wrong,
And e'en amid Oppression's gnashing throng,
He ever walked a kind and genial Friend,
To slave and master faithful to the end.

He stood on Truth's serene and lofty height,
  Clothed with a graceful robe that Heaven gave,
  To wear through life, and fold him in the grave,
That Toil and Battle only made more bright,—
  A robe of finest, firmest tissue wove,

With blended hues of Purity and Love.
From thence, he looked on all the earth around,
And bleeding Brothers every where he found.
For them descending, mingling in the crowd,
His manly form, amid the thickest fight,
Erect with consciousness of sacred Right,
And never lost in Passion's stifling cloud,
Was seen to bear the Holy Banner high,
Till called to add his radiance to the sky.

TO THE GREEK SLAVE.

Hail, child of Genius, Grecian Maid!
  Thy mournful story we have heard;
Thy beauty here, thy woe portrayed,
  The world's deep sympathy has stirred.
The haughty Turk made thee his slave,
  But dreamed not that his cruel wrong,
Denying thee a welcome grave,
  Would curse him in this marble song.

'T is true, no tears are on thy cheek,
  Nor tremble in th' averted eye,—
Thy speechless agony doth seek
  Despair,—it has no voice to cry.

Thy bosom hath a grief too sore
  For aught but silence to express;
If Pity now thou would'st implore,
  'T is Heaven, not Earth, thou would'st address.

A Father once, with swelling heart,
  Beheld thy maiden charms unfold,
Nor dreamed that e'er the Sculptor's art
  Would his fair child a captive mould;
A Mother fondly cherished thee,
  With purest love that mortals know,
Nor dreamed that all the world would see,
  In marble wrought, her daughter's woe.

Go forth, upon thy mission high;
  Tell what a Tyrant man can be,—
Go where thy sable sisters sigh,
  In this dear land of Liberty!
Although as white as lilies are,
  As white and pure as virgin snow,

Thy forehead wreathed with auburn hair,
  And roses might have bloomed below;

Perhaps thy silent woe may wake
  A Nation's conscience, once so free,
And hearts of coldest marble shake,
  With throbs of human sympathy;
Perhaps the Master may behold
  In thee his fearful crime portrayed,
Reminded of the girl he sold,
  To swell the heartless Pirate's trade.

Perhaps the tears he saw her shed,
  When torn from all she loved on earth,—
The tears that his own children fed,
  That gemm'd their brows, and bought them mirth,—
Will trickle from thy marble eyes,
  While he shall fondly gaze on thee,
And, softened, to his own surprise,
  Wonder how he so base could be.

What, though so dark her velvet skin,
  And crisp and curled her raven hair,
There beats her rounded breast within,
  A heart as lily maiden's fair.
God loves her quite as well as you,
  Ye daughters of the vainly proud!
And when her pilgrimage is through,
  She 'll shine as bright in Angel crowd.

Why, then, should she be tortured here?
  Why trodden under brutal feet,
Deprived of all we hold most dear,
  Denied the boon to us so sweet?
Perhaps, ere long, to his dismay,
  The mystery will be explained;
The Tyrant, then, may vainly pray
  To dwell with those he once disdained.

TO THE SAME.

Ah, lovely Maid! thy injured charms
  To brutal gaze exposed,
Despair, succeeding first alarms,
  The tear-springs sadly closed,—
No wonder that the stone, though hard and cold,
By Pity moved, from ancient slumber rolled,
And caught thy beauty ere it passed
  Into the Tyrant's grasp;
For dear the chains that hold thee fast,
  Compared with his rude clasp.

The chilly fetters hug thy form,
As if to kindly shield,
From men with shameless passion warm,
Who ne'er to mercy yield.
Ah! what a shudder soon will thrill thy frame,
When he, the guilty Buyer, shows his claim,
And roughly shall unclasp those links,
That bind thee safely there,
Unheeding how thy spirit sinks
In depths of dark despair.

As when the bird by fowler snared,
Of fruitless struggle tired,
Lies quietly, for death prepared,
The captive hour expired,
Trembles anew when near the hunter brings,
His hand, to loose the cords that bind her wings,—
So thou wilt tremble when the chains
Release their harmless hold,

And thou shalt feel how sternly reigns
Who buys thee with his gold.

Our mountains sent a soldier brave,
To avenge thy country's wrongs;
He saw thy brothers' banner wave,
And shared the victor's song.
Here happy Genius rocked his cradle too,
Who made thy beauty deathless, and thy woe.

Alas! our pity turns to shame,
For he who wronged thee, Maid,
Of Freedom scarcely knew the name,—
We blush while we upbraid:
For here thy sister is compelled to stand,
Before the Tyrant's gaze, in Freedom's land,
And bare to Brutes her virgin breast,
Their insolence endure,
And, silent, pass the rudest test,
Though innocent and pure.

No matter how her soul may shrink
From trial so severe,
The meanest monsters dare to think
Their right to her is clear;
No earthly arm can interpose its power
To help the maiden in that fearful hour.

Her Father dare not lift a hand,
To shield his child forlorn,
The Mother must her tears command,
And let her heart be torn;
The Lover dare not raise a cry
Of anguish at the sight,
And would be murdered should he try
To save his heart's delight.
How, then, can *we* of others' wrongs complain,
To whom *four million slaves* appeal in vain?

"It doth not appear what we shall be."

Though veiled our eyes, and dim our sight,
And darkly shrouds us, Nature's Night,
We walk by Faith's unclouded light.

Though Grief her mantle o'er us flings,
And earthly joys unfold their wings,
Seraphic Hope still sweetly sings.

Afflictions here, if understood,
From seeming evil, change to good,
Their bitter dregs, to richest food.

We claim no favors from the great, '
The sons of Pride, and men of state,
Whom power, or wealth, or fame inflate.

The Mighty God, enthroned on high,
Who built the earth, and arched the sky,
Has turned on us a Father's eye.

That Eye, that every fear allays,
We meet with humble, filial gaze, •
While heart and lips o erflow with praise.

E'n here, we taste His changeless love,
The earnest sweet of bliss above,
While o'er us broods the Spirit Dove.

He leads us by the waters still,
He feeds us on the verdant hill,
Or vale, where flows the purling rill.

The sons of God His image bear,
Adoption's spirit breathes this prayer,
Hereby we know what now we are.

'T is true, it doth not yet appear
Just what we *shall* be,—mortal ear
Could not the wondrous story hear.

But this we know,—that when we see
Fulfilled our Father's last decree,
Our souls shall be forever free.

When Jesus shall in clouds descend,
To make of Sin and Death an end,
He 'll greet us as a loving Friend.

No mist shall then our sight obscure;
Our vision clear, of Truth secure,
Shall see the Beautiful and Pure.

With rapture full, and ever new,
Our glorious Savior we shall view,
And, brightest hope! be *like* Him too.

"The Angel of the Lord encampeth round about them that fear Him."

Methinks I see an Angel band,
  In snowy tents encamping round;
The shining seraphs near me stand,
  I hear their wings' low, rustling sound.

They 've come to guard me when I sleep,
  To guide my wanderings while I wake,
To gently soothe me when I weep,
  And burdens from my spirit take.

How kindly beam their heavenly eyes,
  When hovering o'er my fevered bed,

They breathe again my bosom's sighs,
And fan my weary, aching head.

The host of Hell in vain assails
The soul with such attendants blest;
The rage of man as surely fails
To reach the Angel-guarded breast.

E'en Death, who seems to conquer all,
Must yield his victim to their care;
They watch, and at the temple's fall,
The spirit to its God they bear.

What terrors, then, hath Death for me,
If I may rest in Angel arms?
Should not my eyes delight to see,
Unveiled, their pure and spotless charms?

Those holy Guardians rightly scorn
All earthly ranks, distinctions vain;

They serve as well the slave forlorn,
Nor sooner soothe the monarch's pain.

The beggar's eyes, when closed on earth,
Angelic forms do often greet;
And men of proud and princely birth
No brighter escort ever meet.

How sweet to feel, that not alone
We travel through this chilly world;
However humble or unknown,
The Angel banner ne'er is furled.

Our path may lie along the heights,
Where Heaven's sunbeams always play,
Our presence there the Camp invites,
To guide us on the shining way.

And if our journey leads us where
The shadows gather darkest Night,

The silver tents are 'round us there,
  And gild the gloom with starry light.

Perhaps, O sweet, delightful thought!
  If we could see their radiant forms,
Familiar features would be caught,
  Blending the old with new-born charms.

Perhaps, ah, what a blessed hope!
  We yet may join the cherub throng,
To guide the Loved, who still may grope
  This shadowy pilgrimage along.

LIFE.

Our Life is ever flowing,
  Like a never-sleeping stream,
And none are ever knowing
  When shall wake the pleasing dream.

The Past is all receding,
  Like the shadow of a cloud;
Our steps are ever leading
  From the cradle to the shroud.

Fond memories are thronging,
  Of the path we leave behind,

And still we feel a longing
  For a Good we do not find.

The Now, however pleasant,
  To the Future do we flee;
However sweet the Present,
  There is sweeter yet to be.

The music of the Angel
  That is singing in our breast,—
The Spirit's sweet evangel,—
  With the whispers of the Blest,

Are telling us of Beauty,
  Where the Shadows never play,
And winning us to Duty,
  As we speed us on our way.

The Lofty and the Lowly
  Are descending to the Plain;

The Humble and the Holy
  Are the brightest of the Train.

Our baubles we are leaving,
  On the billows floating by,
So busy are we weaving
  Us a mantle for the sky.

Though Passion is decaying,
  And our senses growing dull,
We heed not their betraying
  Of the soon forsaken hull.

The Pilot-boat is nearing,
  And the Haven is at hand,
The crystal cliffs appearing
  Of the longed-for Better Land.

"Our Father which art in Heaven."

Above the jewelled sky, beyond the stars,
Where mortal vision never yet has reached,
There dwells Our Father,—He who only breathed,
And we, His children, into being sprang,
And clay became the wonderful abode
Of living spirits, that can never die.
Yes, we who grope and grovel in the dust,
As if we had no other life, and Earth
Was parent of our souls, the Pilgrim's span,
The measure of our being,—even such
May look upon the stars with eyes of Faith,
And feel that they shall twinkle yet beneath
Our feet,—that God will let us dwell in Heaven,
And own the humblest of us as His child.

"Take heed that ye despise not one of these little ones."—Matt. xvii. 10.

Despisest thou that little tiny form,
  The most defenceless of all living things,
That hardly could endure the chilly storm,
  As safely as the bird with half-fledged wings?
That lies so helpless in its mother's arms,
  A butterfly might fan its breath away,
Revealing but to her its doubtful charms,
  The weakest, frailest bud of yesterday?
Beware! that feeble thing is dearer far
  To God, than all the treasured wealth of earth!
He never planted in its sphere a star
  To be compared a moment with its worth,
And rather would He sweep a world away,
Than let that little spirit cease to be.

No sooner did that heart begin to beat,
  And God had breathed upon the throbbing clay,
Than Guardian Angels, on their pinions fleet,
  Were sent to guide the little Pilgrim's way.
Before the Father's face they ever stand,
  Radiant with kindly, holy sympathy,
And prompt to heed and do His least command,
  To keep from harm the little stranger free.
I know not what the Bright Ones do in Heaven,
  Or on what other holy mission sent;
Perhaps they trim the silver lamps of Even,
  Or nursing flowers their sweetness oft is spent;
'T is sure, the Infant is allowed to share,
Their gentle love, and never-sleeping care.

How sweet the thought, when folded in her arms,
  The Mother watches, oft with fear oppressed,
Her precious charge unfold its ripening charms,
  That *other* eyes upon the dear one rest!
And when her weary nature yields to sleep,

And she must close her dim, reluctant eyes,
Her babe, as balmy slumbers o'er her creep,
Is guarded by those Heralds of the skies!
If God so loves the helpless little one,
And Angels bright a kindred feeling know,
No wonder that the Father's glorious Son
Should freely let His kind affection flow,
Toward those whose mothers brought them to be
blessed,
And laid their children on the Savior's breast.

THE IDEAL.

In beauty gleaming on my raptured soul,
  I had a sweet Ideal, a vision fair,
Brightness with sweetness flowing o'er the whole,
  As silver clouds may rosy blushes wear.
And, as I looked, I seemed to float along,
  As I were bathing in the purple dawn,
Or gently wafted on the breath of song,
  Over some fragrant, flower-enamelled lawn.
The air was full of fragrance, and my lips
  Seemed steeped with dew, as if I long had slept,
Just where the cloud in the horizon dips,
  Or roses had sweet tears upon me wept,
And o'er me woven, in a balmy bower,
Distilled Ambrosia through the star-lit hour

THE REAL.

The sweetest moment that a mortal knows,
  Ere Angels fold him in their fond embrace,
Is when the Ideal into the Real flows,
  And Substance of the Shadow takes the place:
When Dreams that hold us with so strong a spell,
  And rudely mock us in our waking hours,
Become Realities, and with us dwell,
  As vapors fall in dew upon the flowers.
But who has felt a rapture such as this,
  Or such a joy hath folded in his arms?
Aye! who hath found on Earth so rare a bliss,
  Or called his own such soul-entrancing charms?
He who the Rainbow never vainly grasped,
Or found a Pearl, the dew-drop which he clasped!

MUSIC.

I love the music even of my dreams,
  When on my spirit Angels seem to play;
And when the Dawn awakes its purple gleams,
  How sweetly music greets the opening day!
E'en sultry noon hath only pleasant toil,
  If songs the weary laborer rejoice,
And 'round the heart melodious numbers coil,
  Whether of warbling bird or loved one's voice.
To me 't is sweetest when the Sun declines,
  And folds around him, loose, his robe of gold,
And, lying on his gorgeous couch, resigns
  His realm, that Stars may brief dominion hold:
Music to hush to rest the sleepy light,
And softly usher in the gentle Night.

BEAUTY.

What beauty there is in a dew-drop clear,
As it sparkles bright in a floweret's eye;
More beautiful still is a maiden's tear,
When it trickles down at a sufferer's cry.

How sweet is the light of the evening star,
As it looketh down on the darkened Earth;
But woman's soft eye—it is lovelier far,
When it tenderly beams upon slighted worth.

How graceful the form of the radiant girl,
As she floats in the maze of the waltz's whirl;

But lovelier still is her sister there,
As she bendeth low in the house of prayer.

How bright is the flash of the diamond rare,
As it blends with the light of the festive glare;
But brighter than gems of the house of mirth,
Are the tears that sprinkle the mourner's hearth.

HOPE.

IN YOUTH.

The Bird it is of golden plume,
  That comes in Summer's sunny days,
That gayly trills o'er flower or tomb,
  And with the fluttering leaflet plays.

IN AGE.

The Bird it is of snowy wings,
  That glides through Winter's sparkling air,
Its couplets low and silvery sings,
  On trees, of bloom and foliage bare.

SATURDAY NIGHT.

When all our week-day toil is o'er,
And Evening softly glideth in,
And hushed is labor's busy hum,
The Sabbath doth begin.

It matters not what Law decrees,
Or how the Doctors wise decide,
We feel that Sabbath is begun,
And work is laid aside.

The proper duties of the week,
Performed aright, release their hold,
We number them with things gone by,—
Their story now is told.

With tears for duties unperformed,
With hope that sin has been forgiven,
We wait the dawn of Sabbath morn,—
The ante-type of Heaven.

All other evenings have their cares,
Our restless thoughts keep laboring on,
To-morrow's dawn will wake to toil,
Our rest will soon be gone.

And so we hurry to our sleep,
Or else too soon the light will come;
As o'er us gentle slumber steals,
We list the morrow's hum.

Perhaps unquiet dreams disturb,
Anticipating future toil,
Or what is done we do again,
And thus our comfort spoil.

But now the business of the week
Is finished, and the sweet repose
Of coming Sabbath rest begins,
    And time serenely flows.

We lay our dusty garments by,
Resign ourselves to balmy sleep;
No visions of to-morrow's work
    Among our slumbers creep.

Or if a thought of morrow comes,
While floating toward the land of dreams,
It is a soothing thought, and one
    Of Sabbath's golden gleams.

What quiet raptures thrill the soul,
When, like Æolian, soft and clear,
Some strain of distant music falls
    Upon the raptured ear.

So sweetly float among our thoughts,
The Sabbath scenes that soon shall rise,
To cheer us while we glide along
Our journey to the skies.

ORDINATION HYMN.

Blessed Savior! hear our praises,
  Loud and sweet our song shall be,
Joy its grateful tribute raises,
  Tribute only due to Thee;
    Thou hast sent us
  One with Truth to make us free.

Fount of Life's perennial river,
  Thou, by all to be adored,
Thou, of good the only Giver,
  Glad we own Thee, Gracious Lord!
    Now we thank Thee
  For a Teacher of Thy Word.

Gracious Word, Thyself revealing;
  Richest treasure man can own;
Gently with the contrite dealing,
  Melting oft the heart of stone;
      Thou deservest
  All our praise for this alone.

Still we need the Living Teacher,
  Who will work the golden mine;
Who will show us every feature
  Glowing in the page Divine.
      He is given;
  Hallelujahs now are thine!

ORDINATION WELCOME.

'T is done, the sacred tie is sealed,
  That sweetly binds thee to our hearts;
O may our union richly yield
  The precious fruit that love imparts.

May Christ, our Bishop, kindly deign
  To bless the Pastor and his flock;
The hosts of darkness prowl in vain
  Around the fold, near Zion's Rock.

Dear Brother! thou hast kindly come;
  Our Shepherd may'st thou long abide;

We bid thee make our house thy home,
  Our willing doors are opened wide.

As God His blessings shall bestow,
  Our sweetest joys with thee we 'll share;
And when in sorrow lying low,
  We wish thy sympathizing prayer.

We 'll meet thee oft within these walls,
  The blooming youth, the trembling old;
We 'll listen to thy earnest calls,—
  O may our hearts the message hold!

At bridal altar thou shalt stand,
  In wedlock holy join our youth,
With humble prayer, and utterance bland,
  To seal their vows with heavenly truth.

The parting soul shall list thy prayer,
  Whene'er our panting loved ones die;

And thou shalt kindly lead us where
  Their precious dust must darkly lie.

Should'st thou be stricken, and thy heart
  Shall feel the blow, then we will pray
That God may needed strength impart,
  And brighten e'en the darkest day.

So welcome Brother, Pastor dear,
  Welcome to heart, to hearth and board;
Our earnest prayer may Heaven hear,
  And Angels all our vows record!

HYMNS.

I.

Come, let us sing our Savior's name,
  Who vanquished all our foes;
Let's spread abroad His wondrous fame,
  Who banished all our woes.

Let every light-winged wind that blows,
  Let every blooming flower,
Let every star that brightly glows,
  Join all its heavenly power.

Let orb with orb in sweet accord,
  And Angels all combine,

In chorus swell the charming word,
And ne'er the song resign.

If Heaven's every golden tongue
Should join the hosts of Earth,
E'en then there's music still unsung,
In Jesus's boundless worth.

II.

I love to think of that sweet day,
When Christ unveiled His lovely face,
And dropped upon my heart a ray
Of pure, unshaded loveliness.

'T was sweet for one so full of guilt
To feel that glorious Savior mine ,
To know for me His blood was spilt,
For me He left His throne divine.

And yet, although that time was blest,
  And sweetly o'er my spirit glides,
My heart is oft with sin oppressed,
  A cloud of darkness still abides.

I love to think of that bright day,—
  A day of terrors once to me,—
When Christ shall tear the veil away,
  And let me all His glory see.

SONGS FOR THE CLOSE OF SCHOOL.

I.

'T is meet that we should lift our song
To Him whose throne is in the skies,
To whom our praises all belong,
To whom our hymns should daily rise.

His hand has been our constant stay;
His care has shielded us from harm;
His love has mailed our breast by day;
By night we slept upon His arm.

These transient weeks, that now are gone,
Were sweetly linked with mercies bright;
With bounding hearts we hailed their dawn,
With grateful songs record their flight.

Our joyous circle might have wept
On some beloved Brother's grave,
And Death a Sister might have swept
Beneath its dark and silent wave.

We bless Thee, Father, for this hour,
Those months of love, this night of joy;
Thy goodness claims a nobler power
Than mortal tongues can e'er employ.

The school of Life will soon be o er;
But while we linger may we learn
To love Thee, Father, more and more,
Until our souls to Thee return.

II.

Rosy childhood rushes on,
  Through its few but fragrant years,
Like the blushes of the Dawn,
  That the fleeting cloudlet wears.

Like the merry months of Spring,
  Youthful joys fly swiftly too;
Sober Summer soon will bring
  Sober work for us to do.

School-days soon with us must end;
  Soon we leave this dear retreat,
Where our voices love to blend,
  Where our joys are so complete.

School-mates we shall cease to be;
  Daily task and rival zeal,

Morning greeting, noonday glee,
Fled, with laughter's joyous peal.

Long amid the din of life,
Memory, fond, will linger here ;
Aye, perhaps, amid its strife,
Oft will start the unbidden tear.

We are planting now the seed,
Soon the harvest-time will come ;
Then may God, our Father, lead
All His weary children home.

THE SPRING'S DELAY.

Why tarriest thou, O Spring, these weary days?
Art thou afraid of Winter lurking near?
Will he come back, another tempest raise,
Just as thy leaves and grasses shall appear,
And blast the beauties budding in thy lap?
Art thou afraid that thy new robe of green
Untimely snow will in its mantle wrap,
And cast a chill upon the radiant scene?
I have it—thou would'st not at once unfold
Thy clustering glories to our wondering joy!
Too soon our kindled rapture would grow cold,
Too much of Beauty, seen at once, might cloy.

And so what seem but tantalizing ways,
Are only fond and kindliest delays.

The Sun does not too quickly sweep away
  The shadows of the Night, but paints the East
With lovely heralds of approaching day,
  And slowly is the welcome light increased.
The Evening gently leads its silent hours,
  Revealing, one by one, its jewels rare;
Nor does the rose-bush blaze at once with flowers,
  And in a moment all it blushes wear.
And such, methinks, Eternity must be,
  A sweet unfolding of unfading joys:
Not all of Heaven doth the spirit see,
  When Death at first the shadowy curtain draws.
Oh, no,—when Ages shall have passed away,
The light of Dawn will scarce have ceased to play.

Though no one but the Infinite can bear
  The boundless whole of Heaven's blessedness,

Tis not presumption vain to even dare
  To hope its richest treasures to possess.
As loftier heights we gain, there will appear
  Some brighter glory still, to lure us on;
Each momentary gleam, however clear,
  Of nobler day the faintly blushing dawn.
Aye, God will temper the celestial light
  To suit the growing vision of the Blest;
And though they will not need the soothing Night
  To give unwearied eyes a needless rest,
How sweet to know that brighter e'er will be,
Beyond the Now,—a vast Eternity!

AUTUMN.

How bright is Autumn's fading wreath,
  How clear the bracing air,
How pure the fragrant forest's breath,
  The tinted leaves, how fair!

We seek in vain the lovely flowers,
  The sweet things all are dead;
As passed away the Summer hours,
  Their transient beauty fled.

We miss the birds' delightful song,
  We loved to hear so well;
They 're singing on their journey long,
  In warmer climes to dwell.

The verdant hills are turning brown,
And sere 's the greenest vale ;
Chill snows the mountain summits crown ;
The harvest field is pale.

The jolly black-birds sprinkle round
Their little silver showers ;
No truer Socialists are found,
In bright Utopian bowers.

The squirrels revel 'mong the trees,
And chatter all the day ;
The never-tired honey-bees,
No busier than they.

The whinnering coons, like human thieves,
Asleep at early morn,
Now nightly steal among the sheaves,
Or 'mid the standing corn.

I love our Autumn's bright array,
Its swiftly changing views:
The birches yellow, beeches grey,
The maple's crimson hues.

'o gloomy shadows cast their frown
Upon the cushioned ground;
How gently floats the leaflet down,
How soft its rustling sound.

The vine, that with its branches weaves
A dear, delightful bower,
Reveals, beneath its golden leaves,
Its rich and purple dower.

The Autumn evenings, O how fair!
When stars are shining bright;
How sweet its balmy breezes are,
When bathed in silver light.

WINTER.

Winter is here!
But never fear,
Although his kisses are rude and rough;
He 's very bold,
His lips are cold,
And yet his heart, it is warm enough.

Summer may flaunt,
And Spring may taunt,
And Autumn her fading lips may curl;
They cannot boast
So bright a host
Of rosy cheeks as Winter, my girl.

THE SNOW-FLAKE.

Come hither, Clara, take thy stand,
  And catch that floating flake of snow;
Spread out thy little dimpled hand,
  Tell which is whitest, if you know.

'T is gone! but comes another there;
  Of this be sure, be careful now!
You 've caught the subtle child of air,
  And one has lighted on your brow.

Unclasp your hand, and let me see
  Your pretty captive in its nest;
Bad luck again, my chickadee!
  Too rude the tiny truant 's pressed.

Once more we 'll try, and there is one
  Much larger seems than all the rest;
How bright it sparkles! Oh, well done!
  We truly now are doubly blest.

Was ever aught so clear and white,
  Or aught so beautiful and pure?
But see! the blue and loving light
  Of your soft eyes, it can 't endure.

The life of that I said to you
  Was on your brow, was just as brief;
'T is now a pearly drop of dew,
  Glistening on a lily leaf.

I see one venturing near your lips,
  By those two rose-leaves led astray;
Into the ruby cup it slips
  And in a twinkling melts away.

Now somewhat like these flakes of snow,
The fleeting, cheating joys of Earth;
Dissolved in tears, the purest flow,
The brightest perish in their birth.

One gently floating towards us, seems
Secure, and then eludes our grasp;
Another melts e'en while it gleams,
Or dieth in too rude a clasp.

And yet there is that can bestow
On all that God to us has given,
A bright and never-fading glow,
And tinge e'en Earth with hues of Heaven.

It beauty gives to all that fades,
New life imparts to all that dies,
The fainting spirit kindly aids,
And stills the drooping mourner's sighs.

THE GEM.

There is a gem of priceless worth,
  To every Christian given ;
Unlike the gilded toys of Earth,
  'T is treasured up in Heaven.

'T is there amid its glories grand,
  From thence can ne'er be riven ;
Protected by the very hand
  Through which the nail was driven.

Beyond the reach of wily foes,
  How vain is their endeavor ;

Secure the jewel brightly glows,
  Nor fadeth it forever.

Cornelia, be this treasure thine,
  That none from thee can sever:
Thine *once*, the Savior's love divine,
  And thou shalt perish never.

A LONG RAIN.

A cloudy, muggy, drizzly day,
Oh, what a day is this!
There scarcely seems to be a ray,
To gild the name of bliss.

The substance, too, 't is hard to find,
And hard for home to smile;
O Jewsharp! homely music grind,
The weary hours beguile.

I cannot play on such a day,
For, like the dreary sky,

The Horrors on my spirit weigh,—
  I cannot even try.

I rather, moody, sit and sog,
  And let it drizzle on;
My jaded nag may, dripping, jog,
  Life's muddy road upon.

Is Mother Nature cleaning house,
  And flirting 'round her mop?
Why can't she give her child a souze,
  And then, in mercy, stop?

It seems as if there never would
  A day of sunshine dawn;
That smile again we never could,
  But only sit and yawn.

Oh, if this everlasting cloud
  Would let a little sky

Peep through its rifted, leaden shroud,
  I'd bid the dumps good-by.

I like the rushing, gushing flood,
  That pours in torrents down;
It cheers my heart, and cools my blood,—
  I like the tempest's frown.

But, Oh, these long and gloomy days,
  This lazy, sozzling rain,—
I'd rather wither in the blaze
  That burns the tropic plain.

The water dripping from the eaves,
  In slow, reluctant stream,
The drooping of the weary leaves,—
  How dismal does it seem!

All day, all night, all day, all night,—
  I scarce remember when,

Of Phœbus I have had a sight,
Or of good-natured men.

Last night, I sought my tired bed,
Of course, awake I lay,
And heard till midnight, o'er my head,
It driz-zle-ing away.

At last I fell asleep, and dreamed
Of, Oh, how sweet a dawn!
But waked to find, though day had gleamed,
It still was drizzling on.

The birds, at first, were wondrous glad,
When it began to rain;
They seemed to be all music mad,
Or bent upon a train.

But it is now a week or so
Since I have heard a note;

Perhaps, if we the truth could know,
  Their eggs are all afloat.

Bold Chanticleer, collapsed and tame,
  The meekest of his flock,
No proud preeminence can claim,—
  Poor melancholy cock!

His majesty so taken down,
  His pride and glory gone,
A king who had just lost his crown
  Was never more forlorn.

Of hydrophobia, not a few
  Topers are running mad;
Cold water folks, already blue,
  Their favorite beverage dread.

There goes a dark umbrella by;
  I wonder whose it is;

He crouches under it so sly,
  I doubt if it is his.

I know some one has stolen mine,—
  To use the proper name
For borrowing, without design
  Of bringing back the same.

How slow and carefully he walks,
  How mincingly he goes!
While Patrick like a major stalks,
  And draggled coat-tail tows.

Extemporaneous brooks abound,
  Pedestrians must leap;
Squire Pompous has a river found,
  That 's several inches deep.

Too proud to seek another place,
  Where he can safely wade,

Against the bank I see him brace,—
A desperate leap is made.

I cannot think it is a sin
For me to laugh at him,
To see him sadly taken in,
And be obliged to swim.

It is a streak of sunshine this,
A welcome episode!
So funny looks that dismal face,
Emerging from the mud.

AN OLD MAID.

Beneath the sky there 's nothing better,
Than an old maid to me ;
She spurns the halter, spurns the fetter,—
There is no bird so free.

She could have married, but she would not,
And bravely answered, No ;
She thinks 't is sad that others could not,
An equal courage show.

Through fear if there were not so many,
Who throw themselves away,
She says there never need be any
To curse their wedding day.

The father's pet, the mother's darling,
Their trembling steps she guides;
What though she now and then is snarling,
Good nature still abides.

The brothers all are glad to greet her,
And all the sisters too;
The children, shouting, run to meet her,
Oh, kiss us, Aunty, do!

They find her always very ready
To stay with little Sis;
She is so trusty and so steady,
They nothing find amiss.

Are any sick, there 's none so skilful,
All healing herbs she knows;
And if to Doctors seems so wilful,
And oft his poison throws

Where it can do no tardy killing,
  But massacre his bill,
She keeps her harmless roots distilling,
  While Nature does her will.

At last, some good man's wife, o'erweary,
  Departs this troubled life;
His home will be so dreadful dreary,
  He 'll want another wife.

He has amassed enough of money,
  No need of further toil;
The first, to fill the hive with honey,
  Spared not the midnight oil.

A second wife, an old man's deary,
  No longer an old maid;
Her home so happy, bright and cheery,
  She is glad that she delayed.

TWENTY-FIVE.

Ah, still at home and twenty-five!
 How swift the hasty years roll on,—
It only seems a merry drive,
 Since first I saw life's purple dawn.

And here the "corner" looms in sight,—
 The timid maiden's primal fear;
I would not dodge it, if I might,
 I'll face it with a queenly air.

'T is not so horrid, after all,
 Nor quite so sharp as many fear;

A gentle curve, the place I call,—
  The path ahead seems bright and clear.

Of fellow-pilgrims some are left,
  I do not travel all alone ;
And Love our hearts has never cleft,
  His subtle arrows careless thrown.

A merry company are we,
  With these unburdened hearts of ours ;
As on we float, the shadows flee,
  Our path is fringed with dewy flowers.

'T is true, the simple girl-wife sighs,
  And feels that we her pity need,
Nor dreams that we, too, may have eyes,
  And in her face her sorrows read.

We see her pale and sickly cheek,
  Where many dimples used to play,

When we together used to seek
  Enjoyment through the livelong day.

'T is plain that she has found her hope
  Of happiness a transient dream;
With pain and trouble forced to cope,
  She struggles on Life's turbid stream.

She has discovered, all too late,
  That lovers' vows are soon forgot;
And, though she cannot change her fate,
  In secret mourns her hapless lot.

Ah me! the faces she must wash,
  The ugly garments she must mend,
The quailing 'neath the angry flash
  Of him who vowed to be her friend.

How weary, worn and wan is she!
  There lingers scarcely life enough

To say, "I wish I could be free!"
  Her lot is hard, her road is rough.

At early dawn she flies to toil,
  No time to rest, no time to play;
To skim, to bake, to stew, to boil,
  Complete the round of every day.

The sunlight, stealing through the pane,
  Tries to relieve her weary task;
The birds their carols sing in vain,
  The flowers might well their beauty mask.

The cook-stove is her daily sun,
  The kitchen ceiling bounds her sky,
The kettle sings for her alone,
  In chorus darling children cry.

Her tireless conflict never ends,
  With rats, and dust, and appetite,

To put together odds and ends,
And tumbled furniture to right.

Her mind? alas! she *had* a mind,
But sadly doomed to sore neglect;
To household duties all confined,
What could a heartless world expect?

But still she fain would pity me;
The poor thing tries to start a tear,
And wastes her needless sympathy,
Nor heeds the burden she must bear.

And husbands, vain, will show their wit,
Repeating jests at our expense,
And think it very keen to twit,—
Yet only show their impudence.

But all their pointless darts rebound;
'T is bliss to think their galling chain

Was ne'er our freedom thrown around,
  And we can smile with calm disdain.

Well, worry on, ye gentle ones,
  And wear your weary life away,
In halter-breaking, wayward sons,
  The stubborn daughter's helpless prey.

A home?—my father's home is mine,
  He grudges not a single joy;
My mother's love, almost divine,
  My heart's best sympathies employ.

Of friendships pure I have enough,
  All earthly blessings prized above;
No *one* great surging, whelming wave,
  To wash away all others' love.

I seem about as young, I ween,
  I am as full of joy, I know,

As when I was but "sweet sixteen,"—
  Life's numbers as serenely flow.

The future?—what hath it in store?
  If measured by the rosy past,
It hath of blessings more and more,
  Each richer, sweeter, than the last.

Another corner just ahead?—
  Well, let it come, I'm all prepared
To greet the turn without a dread;
  What *has* been, can again be dared.

Perhaps!—ah, well, I will not give
  The darling thought to babbling words;
But it is true, we always live
  Content while Hope our spirit girds.

A BACHELOR'S FAREWELL TO HIS BED.

As, late at night, he hies to his room,
  His face appears unusually sad;
He walks as if approaching his tomb,
  And Life can never again be glad.

At other times his step was so light,
  It seemed as if he never had known
That naught of Earth can always be bright,
  And thorns among the flowers are strewn.

Though grave his face, beneath it there lay
  A troop of smiles;—to welcome a friend,

They never were reluctant to play,
  As Thought and Feeling would merrily blend.

What ails him now, he looketh so sad?
  What burden heavy loadeth his heart?
Is Fortune angry, making him mad?
  With treasure is he grieving to part?

Oh, no,—he goes to pillow his head,
  Where oft it hath so happily lain;
To bid farewell to his bachelor bed,
  Oh, hear him sigh his bitter refrain:

O precious bed! I come to thee now,
  Once more to be thy occupant lone;
To Fate's decree I mournfully bow,
  For Cupid's dart is fatally thrown.

How many times I have found thee to be,
  Though deaf to others' importunate prayers,

Yet ever kind and ready for me,
  Thy swelling breast, sweet soother of cares.

No grumbling wife came petulant here ;
  No babies cried, and kicked off the clothes ;
I never, crowded, slumbered in fear,
  And naught disturbed my sweetest repose.

If absent, none were here to inquire
  Where I had been, with jealousy seized ;
No call, at morn, to kindle a fire,
  I slept as long as ever I pleased.

No mortal shared thy cushioned domain,
  Thy soft embraces all were my own ;
I never sought thy solace in vain,—
  Alas ! those nights forever have flown.

How sweet the forms that visited me,
  When silent hours I wakefully lay ;

In dreams Elysian, Oh, I was free!
  And let my Fancy revelling play.

I pressed thee warm, and covered me close,
  When Winter's breath was icily cold;
Just left exposed my innocent nose,
  All else enclosed in balmiest fold.

In Summer warm I fearlessly spread,
  Nobody to chide for crowding too far;
I floundered free, with nothing to dread,
  Enough of room, though nothing to spare.

But I must leave thee, bachelor bed!
  The kindling dawn is bidding me haste;
I careless promised a maiden to wed,—
  The music must be manfully faced!

Though now I bid thee a final adieu,
  Do n't think that I shall ever forget

The blessed times I have revelled with you,
  Since long ago we lovingly met.

I know 't is vain for me to repine,
  The fearful step I cannot recall,—
I 'll bravely try to meekly resign,
  And let the noose connubial fall.

THRICE MARRIED.

Again the silken cord has bound
  Another to thy bleeding breast,
And Love again thy heart has found,
  And truly thou art sweetly blessed.

'T is true, the girl so fondly won,
  'Mid fragrant Youth's unfaded bloom,
Her gentle race has long since run,—
  She long has slumbered in the tomb.

You loved her when your heart was strong,
  And beat with Life's young pulses warm;
You fondly wreathed a myriad throng
  Of hopes around her fairy form.

And, Oh, she was so passing fair!
  So pure and angel-like she seemed,
So sweet a smile she used to wear,
  Of other Heaven you scarcely dreamed.

'T were vain to paint the vision bright,
  That gently gleamed upon us all;
With chilly words to drape the light
  That bound us with so sweet a thrall.

One might as wisely try to tell
  Whence is the rose's magic power,
Or why it hath a stronger spell
  Than any other earthly flower.

And yet she lived a painful life;
  Her form the fearful battle-ground,
Where fierce diseases waged a strife,
  Which could inflict the deepest wound.

We often think with wonder how
  She kept her soul so calm and sweet,
While anguish plowed her sunny brow,
  And torture pulsed in every beat.

But did you ever hear a word
  Of sore complaint, impatient, fall?
Was ever bitter feeling stirred,
  To wrap her spirit in its pall?

From those blue eyes did other rays
  Than Love's serenest ever flow?
Or ever dimmed with other haze
  Than that of tears, did'st ever know?

And now it is the dearest bliss
  That you may gather from the past,
None dearer can there be than this:
  She loved you fondly to the last,—

Unless, perchance, it is to think
  How much you did to soothe her pain,—
How faithful to the very brink,
  From whence she joined the angel train.

And she who took your Mary's place,
  And brought a heart so warm and true,
Who bore with such a winning grace
  The name of wife and mother too.

I need not call her virtues o'er,
  Nor mind you of her precious worth;
I need not tell the love she bore
  For every living thing of earth.

How much she did to bless your home,
  What tireless energy she had!
How wide her sympathy would roam,
  To make some stranger-spirit glad!

The more the sorrowing shared her love,
  The fuller seemed the fount to be;
The more her charity would rove,
  The closer did she cling to thee.

Ah, noble woman! few are they
  Who ever richer graces wear;
Not often doth serener ray
  The brow of living mortal bear.

The elastic step, and comely form,
  The gushing laugh, the swimming eye,
The words that flowed from heart so warm,—
  Oh, they can never, never die!

And then to God and Good how true!
  How worshipped she Eternal Right!
How fondly gazed on Heaven's blue,
  How dear to her its golden light!

And dear to her were those you loved,
  Your every joy by her was shared ;
Just like a mother sweetly moved,
  And yours like children ever fared.

And now, dear Friend, we all are sure
  That God for thee had kindest thought,
For He hath helped thee to secure
  A kindred heart to bless thy lot.

Her modesty would not permit
  My bungling pen to now portray
The radiance that has kindly lit
  The shades of thy declining day.

May He, whose hands our ways control,
  Allow the rod a long repose ;
In mercy may Life's numbers roll,
  And slowly waft thee to its close.

NOT HIDDEN.

The silver haze
The moon betrays,
Though veiled her virgin breast;
She coyly stays,
With fond delays,
Then shows her shining crest.

So Love is shy,
And fain would try
To hide the pleasing wound;
The tender sigh,
And beaming eye,
Unbidden, tell the tale around.

IN AN ALBUM,

OPPOSITE A PICTURE OF "THE ELDER SISTER."

Thine Elder Sister! who is she?
Pray, tell who can the creature be?
She does not seem so very old,
And if it would not be too bold,
On ladies' age to speculate,
I'd say she may be twenty-eight.
Her heart is sound,
As I'll be bound,
For Cupid's wound
Would take the round
Out of that cheek, so full, so fresh, so soft, so fair,—
E'en sweet sixteen a brighter bloom doth seldom wear.

Some people's lips are very thin,
And white, as if made out of tin;
Thy Sister's still are full and red,
And doubtless sweetest fragrance shed;
        And if the Bee
    The rosy things should see,
    As plainly as do we,
        It seems to me,
        She soon would fly,
        And boldly try
To find what sweets lie hidden there,—
A deed that I should never dare.

TO ——.

You say you are a Mother,
  That a Pearl is on your breast;
That never was another
  With an equal treasure blest.

Beneath their silken lashes,
  That such eyes were never seen;
You think their magic flashes
  From the stars our gaze should wean.

You deem that wondrous pretty
  Is that little baby-boy;
That others need your pity,
  Who would claim an equal joy.

Perhaps he'll set the river
All a-blazing, when a man;
His country may deliver,
As successor of Buchan.

Perhaps he will discover
What the wise have sought in vain;
All hidden truths uncover,
And all mysteries explain.

I 'm sure perpetual motion
He will easily unfold;
Perhaps will take a notion
To be changing dust to gold.

He charcoal may be turning
Into diamonds now so rare,
That Queens may soon be spurning
What they now so proudly wear.

Will build a ship, and man it,
  And be sailing through the air,
And, visiting some planet,
  Will its ancient fogies scare.

Perhaps will be another,
  Not unlike the rest of us,
A good and loving Brother,
  Who will make but little fuss.

Forgive this last suggestion,
  If it seems to you absurd,—
Till Time shall solve the question,
  Let your vengeance be deferred.

I cannot help insisting,
  That before there may have been,
In baby-blanket twisting,
  As remarkable a scene.

TO A BRIDE.

I saw thee in thy mother's arms,
Lie nestling there in sinless charms,
Her loving smile a Heaven to thee,
And thine to her, 't was plain to see.

I saw thee on thy father's knee,
Fearless amid the careless glee,
With tiny grasp fend off the nose,
That far before his kisses goes.

I saw thee climb the dizzy height,
And on thy brother's shoulder light,

Too far for many a bird to fly,
That fain its new-fledged wing would try.

I saw thee with thy sisters dear,
So happy and so fond appear,
That others' love could find no part,
Unoccupied, of thy young heart.

And yet, I see thee listening now,
With blushes mantling e'en thy brow,
To One's beguiling words of love,—
Thy heart is fluttering, captive dove!

And now, upon this bridal night,
I see thee robed in spotless white;
The rose and lily, struggling, seek
The mastery of thy dimpled cheek.

I see him clasp thy trembling hand,
As you before the Altar stand,

And silent pledge the heart to heart,
Till Death the silver cord shall part.

I see thee now a happy Wife,
Beloved and loving, blissful life!
With girlhood's radiance on thy face,
Mingled with woman's pensive grace.

'T is thus, dear Minnie, I have seen,
Of all the Past the tinted sheen;
I would not lift the sacred veil
That hides the yet unwritten tale.

With Hope we murmur, Fare thee well!
With wishes more than lips can tell;
Thy Home, thy Friends, must yield thee now;
To Fate's behest we trustful bow.

TO A YOUNG MOTHER.

Dost thou remember, while a child,
What tender chords were sweetly thrilled
By mortals' richest, dearest word?
What kindly feelings oft were stirred,
Within thy joyful, careless breast,
Toward her by thee thus oft addressed?

Can'st call to mind her look of love,
Changeless as stars that watch above,
Tearful and anxious, chiding, kind?
How day by day she watched thy mind
Unfold its life, its fragrance sip,
Repaying all with dewy lip?

As flew along those light-winged years,
Did'st ever, dreaming, strangely gaze
Upon thyself, a mother too?
Did'st ever see two eyes of blue,—
Of sparkling blue,—look up and long
For Mother's smile, for Mother's song?

Well, such thou art, my gentle girl!
Gleams on thy breast a priceless pearl,
A bright and blue-eyed little Boy!
We wish thee now unmingled joy.
My wife, my heart how sweetly near,—
But Mother of my Boy, how dear!

MY FATHER.

On dark Wyoming's bloody ground there lay
  Her murdered husband, with the mangled dead;
  And fearfully her orphan group she led,
Through the deep woods, upon her lonely way.
Oh! who can weigh the load of grief she bore,
  Expecting every moment to become
The helpless prey of savages, who tore
  Away the Guardian of her babes and home?
My childhood grasped the honest, toil-worn hand
Of him, the youngest of that trembling band;
  God kindly shielded his defenceless years,
  And, mindful of his Mother's burning tears,
Stamped on his brow the seal of noblest worth;
To me he seemed the manliest of Earth!

HOW DID HE LOOK WHEN HE WAS YOUNG?

I asked my aged Mother how
  My Father looked when he was young.
  She loving glances toward me flung,
And answered, " Just as he does now !"

But, Mother dear, that cannot be;
  His form is bent, his locks are white,
  His step is trembling, once so light.
" My son, he looks the same to me !"

But, Mother, had n't he raven hair,
  Like mine, that seems to please you so?
  Or was it always like the snow?
" The blackest locks he used to wear."

His cheek, was it not full and round,
And had he not a sunny brow,
As smooth, you say, as mine is now?
"A fairer forehead ne'er was found."

And had he not a form erect,
A firm, elastic, bounding gait,
With a blithe fairy for his mate?
"My son, your words are all correct."

And did he always look so grave,
And always have that quiet way,
So solemn, thoughtful, never gay?
"His smiles, like ripples on the wave."

Then, Mother, tell me, frankly, how
My Father looked, at twenty-three.
But still she archly smiled on me,
And answered, "Just as he does now!"

I left a kiss upon her cheek,
    And treasured up her sweet reply;
    I saw the love-light in her eye,
And could no other answer seek.

They had grown old, together old:
    They had not marked the slow decay,
    Or noticed, on their loving way,
The change that Time and care had told.

My Father's sight was never dim,—
    Though furrows deep on Mother's face,
    Of dimples had assumed the place,
Yet were they dimples still to him.

My Mother had a deep blue eye,
    And Age could not its sweetness veil;
    But Father's changes did she fail
To see, and o'er them vainly sigh.

"THERE COMES MY GOOD OLD MOTHER."

When on his bed the sufferer lay,
Wasting his weary life away,
Too patient ever to complain,
Enduring never-resting pain.
He turned his gentle, loving eye
Toward the door that opened nigh,
Then sweetly smiled,—my darling Brother,—
And sighed, "There comes my good old Mother!"

When Summer grass began to wave
Upon the loved one's new-made grave,
Mother and I in sadness sought,

With flowing tears, the sacred spot;
When toward the lowly mound we went,
As if the turf a whisper sent,
We heard the voice of sleeping Brother
Repeat, "There comes my good old Mother!"

A few years later, and we bore
Our Mother to the silent shore;
With heavy hearts, we trod the ground,
Broken with many a wavy mound;
And while, in sorrow, we drew near,
In loving tones, we seemed to hear
A greeting from the grave of Brother,
That said, "There comes my good old Mother!"

We laid to rest the sleeping dust,
And Earth received the sacred trust;
Though sad to us that mournful day,
Before we joined their lifeless clay,

A Spirit hailed her from the sky,
Without a tear, without a sigh,—
And lo! she heard my angel Brother
Shouting, "Here comes my good old Mother!"

MY BROTHER.

Dear Brother, hast thou fled,
And left us weeping here?
Oh, must we number with the dead
Whom we have held so dear?

Oh, is it not a sleep
Hath stolen o'er thee now?
Still may we not our vigils keep?
Still fan thy fevered brow?

Wilt thou not join again
Our fond, fraternal band?

O Brother, must we press in vain
Thy damp and chilly hand?

How still his bosom lies!
How still the heart within!
We from his mild and lovely eyes
No glances now can win!

Alas, how pale his cheek!
A leaflet, floating by,
More quiet rest could nowhere seek
Than his cold lips supply.

They tell me thou art gone,
And yet I feel thee near;
Although thy spirit hence has flown,
Thine image lingers here.

Thy body soon must sleep
Low in its native earth;

But still my heart shall fondly keep,
Enshrined, thy cherished worth.

Sweet Brother, fare thee well!
Our loss is all thy gain;
No mortal tongue thy joys can tell,—
This only soothes our pain.

Our days will soon be gone;
We soon shall sleep with thee;
For us the morning soon shall dawn
Of bright Eternity!

TO MY BOY.

Be brave, my boy!
God loathes the coward, loves the brave;
Though Wrong would win thee to its side,
Or whelm thee 'neath its angry wave,
Heed not the proud and foaming tide.
Be brave, my Boy!

Be pure, my Boy!
Passion, of holy love the nurse,
Our Heavenly Father kindly gave
To bless His children, not to curse;
Be thou its master, not its slave.
Be pure, my boy!

Be just, my Boy!
Rather endure the foulest wrong,
And covet torture's keenest thrill,
Than bear the consciousness along
That one, from thee, has suffered ill.
Be just, my Boy!

Be true, my Boy,
To every trust in thee reposed,
To God and to Humanity;
That when thy pilgrimage is closed,
No broken faith may follow thee.
Be true, my Boy!

Be wise, my Boy!
A shroud around thy soul to wind,
The sordid world may proffer gold;
Thy treasure an immortal mind,
Refuse the tempting bribe to hold.
Be true, my Boy!

Be free, my Boy!
The world has truckling slaves enough;
The Many fawn around the Few;
The path of Liberty is rough;
But travel there, thy journey through.
Be free, my Boy!

Be kind, my Boy!
Be good to every living thing,
To kindred and to strangers too;
A bounteous fragrance 'round thee fling,
As sweet, unselfish flowers do.
Be kind, my Boy!

Love, my Boy!
You cannot help but love the Fair;
But *Men*, be not ashamed to love;
A Brother's smile be proud to wear,
For all beneath thee, all above.
Yes, love, my Boy!

Hate, my Boy!
Hate not thy fellows, but their crimes;
Oppression loathe, corruption scorn,
Though Vice to lofty station climbs,
And Virtue mourns a lot forlorn.
Hate, my Boy!

Play, my boy!
Let boys and girls be thy delight;
In genial mirthfulness excel;
And even when thy locks are white,
Do not seal up the living well.
Play, my Boy!

Work, my Boy!
This life demands unceasing toil;
Jehovah works, and Angels too;
Be not afraid thy hands to soil;
What God commands fail not to do.
Work, my Boy!

And laugh, my Boy!
While Joy presents her brimming cup,
When Wit arouses merry thought,
And Pleasure pure is welling up,
And you can laugh as well as not,—
Why, laugh, my Boy!

But weep, my Boy!
Tears are the wealth of noble souls;
When Sorrow claims thy sympathy,
Or thine own grief thy heart controls,
'T is manly,—set the fountain free.
Aye, weep, my Boy!

Watch, my Boy!
Be wide awake! for perils lurk
Around the fairest, brightest path;
Amid thy play, amid thy work,
The Tempter's smile, the Tempter's wrath.
Watch, my Boy!

And pray, my Boy!
The Son of God was wont to pray;
And thou hast need of constant prayer,
That Heaven may thy spirit stay,
And keep thy soul from every snare.
Oh, pray, my Boy!

GERTIE.

"I put my baby into the hands of Jesus, and He took her. I am as certain of it as if I saw Him with my natural sight."

Words of a bereaved young Mother.

I.

My cup of happiness was full, I thought,
  When God bestowed on me a noble breast,
Wherein such worth and constant love were wrought
  That all my spirit-cravings seemed at rest.
His manly form, illumined with a soul
  So rich, and throbbing with a heart so warm,
And all my own,—I fondly deemed my whole
  Of life was bound within his circling arm.
Amid my raptures, came another joy,
  So new, so strangely sweet, I raised my eyes,

Amazed, my lips refusing to employ
  Cold words, and sought where, in the skies,
The rosy smile was playing, whence had come
So dear a gift to bless our happy home!

II.

Ere this, our mutual love we thought supreme,
  But higher, deeper, holier far it seemed,
Our life more real now, and less a dream,
  When Heaven's jewel on my bosom gleamed.
Our ever-deepening raptures to complete,
  With golden ringlets Gertie's head grew bright,
And recognition woke, in smiles so sweet,
  Her laughing eyes so full of merry light,
We tried to kiss the dimples from her cheek,
  But found our kisses only multiplied
The wily things,—as those who eager seek
  To sip the trembling dew, but spread it wide
Upon the blushing leaf;—ah, precious child,
How dear the months thy fragrant life beguiled!

III.

'T is true, amid our joys, there now and then
  Would creep a chilling fear, that God had lent,
Not given,—and that He might take again
  The priceless treasure He had kindly sent.
We thought how easy it would be for Him
  To still the pulses of that little heart,
With snowy wings those dimpled arms to trim,
  And bid the plumed angel to depart.
But gushing from her lips the warbling came,
  That, like a bird's untaught, in silver notes,
Dispelled our rising fears,—as oft the flame
  Revives, when some sweet breeze upon it floats.
We clasped her closer, and we failed to see
The hand that came to set our Gertie free.

IV.

The power of Faith I scarcely knew before,
  The humblest Christian's faith;—before it melt

The tempests into music; and the roar
  Of Thunders, else so fearful, now is felt
A deep vibration of celestial strings;
  Fierce Lightning's flash as harmlessly as smiles;
And Death, to Nature dreadful, only wings
  Our loved ones from the Tempter's deadly wiles.
So when Disease our darling Gertie grasped,
  And all her warbling changed to piteous moans,
Although my heart was breaking, then I clasped
  Her in my trembling arms, and, 'mid our groans,
I handed her to Jesus, and He took
Her, as the Ocean takes the rippling brook.

V.

I saw Him fold her on His ample breast,—
  And, Oh, she hung there like a little star,
And looked so pure, so bright, supremely blest,
  I almost wished I could be with her there!
I saw Him? Yes, amid our flowing tears,—

Amid the crushing agonies of Death,—
Amid our struggling hopes, and surging fears,—
I saw Him gently hush her panting breath!
I am not dreaming,—if these eyes of mine
Had seen my Savior take our Gertie home,
Had heard His voice, beheld His form divine
Ascending with her through the azure dome,
The bright beholding would have failed to be
More real than the vision was to me.

VI.

Amid our desolation, now I ask,
For what our Gertie dear was sent to Earth?
The answer, too, demands no doubtful task:
'T was not alone that she might here have birth;
'T was not because our Father loves to wound,—
To give a joy that He may take away,—
To proffer bliss, and dash it to the ground,—
To make alive, because He loves to slay.

Oh no,—the Shepherd takes the bleating lamb
That He may win the mother to His fold,—
The fragrant field might lure the careless dam,
And in apparent safety growing bold,
She might be lost;—and thus, lest we should roam,
The Shepherd GAVE, and TOOK OUR GERTIE HOME.

LITTLE HENRY.

O Henry! is the grave
Thy cold and silent bed?
Has Death its dark and chilly wave
Rolled o'er thy youthful head?

Oh, has thy sparkling eye
Lost its last lovely ray?
Oh, could its light, so joyous, die,
And fade from Earth away?

Where are the merry tones
We used to hear from thee?

Oh, fled they with the softened moans
That set thy spirit free?

And can it be that Death
Has crushed a Father's joy?
And torn from her who gave him birth,
Her bright and gentle Boy?

Could not the fond embrace
Of Brothers, Sisters, Friends,
With bloom relume thy pallid face,
Thy precious life defend?

Ah, no! if forests bend
Before the sweeping blast,
So frail a flower a breath may rend,
Though gently o'er it passed!

Thy smiles shall gladness ne'er
Our loving circle lend;

With ours thy voice, so sweet and clear,
Its bird-like music blend.

And yet 'tis sweet to know,
Thy heart has never bled;
That Earth withheld her every wo,—
In joy thy years have sped.

We love to think how God
Softened thy dying hour,
And sweetened thus the bitter rod
That smote our lovely flower.

And, Oh, 'tis yet more sweet
To know that Heaven is thine;
Farewell, dear Henry! we shall meet,—
And soon,—in Realms Divine!

HELEN'S BIBLE;

THE GIFT OF A SICK MOTHER.

I.

The starry light
Of Nature's night
But twinkled in the brightest Age;
How clear and white,
And Heaven-bright,
The rays that gild the sacred page!

II.

This precious Book,
With loving look,
Thy gentle Mother fondly gave;

No shepherd's crook,
By rippling brook,
E'er led a lamb to purer wave.

III.

The sweetest rill
From Zion's hill
Presents its crystal waters here ;
Oh, drink at will,
And feel the thrill
Of new-born hope, and joy sincere!

IV.

A silken band
Thy mother's hand
Hath coiled around thy youthful heart;
The Spirit-Land
Will soon command
The dear one from her child to part.

V.

Oh, let her see
Thy spirit free
From Earth's beguiling, fatal power;
And then will she,
So dear to thee,
With rapture hail the closing hour!

PRAYER FOR E——.

Hear, O Father, hear our prayer;
Do our precious darling spare;
Bid the Spoiler leàve his prey,
Send relentless Death away!

Frail she is, as Summer flower,
Bending in the dewy hour,
With its little pearl o'erweighed,
Trembling in the leafy shade.

Fierce Disease has laid her low;
Fever's scarlet embers glow;

Helpless, panting, there she lies,
While the crimson torture plies.

Father, furl that banner red,
Herald of the Spoiler's tread,
Mounted where the flush of health
Lately spread its dimpled wealth.

It is not that she is fair,—
If an angel, she would wear
Brighter, sweeter loveliness
Than on Earth doth mortals bless;

It is not because her voice
Makes our weary hearts rejoice,
Warbling like a happy bird,
With the Summer beauty stirred;

It is not that we should be
Ever from affliction free,

While so many weepers tread,
'Mong so many treasured dead.

Oh, we love her, and we long
Still to hear her merry song;
Life without her will be drear,—
Let us, Father, keep her here.

Plead we not our worthless name;
Own we all our guilt and shame;
If our dear one should be slain,
None could rightfully complain.

Kindly hear our trembling cry;
Do not let our darling die;
In the name of Jesus, we
Offer up our prayer to Thee.

On Thy grace we would rely,
While we train her for the sky,

Guided by the Savior's hand,
Toward the blissful Spirit-Land.

What already Thou hast done,
Since this sorrow hath begun,
We will hope may not be lost,
Till the river we have crossed.

We will love Thee more and more,
While we linger on the shore;
And will prove Thy chastening rod
Hath but driven us to God.

TO JULIA.

Sister, thou hast come again;
  Gladly do we meet thee;
Still, of parting all the pain
  Saddens while we greet thee.

Would that we could keep thee here,
  Never more to wander;
Then would each successive year
  Make us ever fonder.

Here thy loving kindred dwell,
  Fondly thee to cherish;

Strangers cannot keep so well
  Ties that never perish.

Let the sky that smiled on thee
  When a happy maiden,
Evermore thy treasure be,
  With its jewels laden.

Leave the noisy Western world,
  Leave the prairie ocean;
Long enough thy life has whirled
  In its wild commotion.

Stay and nestle in our love,
  Now that Age is creeping;
From the graves no longer roam
  Where thy babes are sleeping.

Bid our Brother hither come,
  Where his young heart found thee;

Win him to the olden home,
  Where his young love bound thee.

In the presence of the hills,
  With their valleys blended,
Soothed by sweetly flowing rills,
  Let thy days be ended.

Would you olden joys partake?
  Linger by these fountains;
Stay in sight of yonder Lake,
  Mirror of the mountains.

Sister, let our final sleep
  Be with Father, Mother;
Let us all together keep,
  Slumbering with each other.

Lying on the breezy hill,
  Grass our bed adorning,

Fearless of the Evening chill,
  Waiting for the Morning.

Sleeping all together there,
  All together waking,
Meeting Jesus in the air,
  When the Day is breaking.

TO LIBBIE.

I have written in many an Album, dear Lib;
And yet have I never recorded a fib,
When wishing for blessings on ruby-lipped girls,
With dimples, and roses, and glittering curls.

Aye, thus did I scribble ere Time, the old fox!
Had stolen the brightness from once raven locks;
When Life was all hopeful, unburdened with care,
The Present unclouded, the Future all fair.

And now on the summit of Life's brief ascent,
A pilgrim aweary, I spread out my tent,
To warble awhile to the swift-rushing gale,
Ere downward I plunge to the star-lighted vale.

The Spring-time is thine yet—the Spring-time so sweet,
Whose flowers are so fragrant, whose days are so fleet;
Oh, may its bright blossoms their purpose fulfil,
Unharmed by the blast, or the frost's stealthy chill!

May Summer not whelm, with her radiant flood,
But ripen and perfect the sweet tinted bud;
May Autumn, amid her pale foliage, show
Rich clusters to gladden her fast-fading glow.

When Winter approacheth, to spread the light sheet,
To guard the chilled Earth from the thickening sleet,
Oh, safe be the roof that shall shelter thy form,
With red-glowing hearth, that shall laugh at the storm.

As onward thou fliest, there 'll now and then be
A burden, a care, and a sorrow for thee;
But He who hath called thee will ever be near,
To guide thee, to help thee, to comfort and cheer.

Too soon wilt thou, Libbie, depart from our Isle;
We vainly shall seek for thy gladdening smile;
But oft as thine eye shall revert to the past,
Oh, let not our Island be thought of the last.

Oh, think of the wavelet's low, murmuring sound,
As it gracefully yields to its pebbly bound;
Remember the billow's bright, silvery spray,
As it lashes the rock that doth keep it at bay.

Oh, yes, Libbie, think of our sweet-scented groves,
Where twineth the vine round the maple she loves;
Where earliest bloometh the violet blue,
Where later the red leaves the mosses bestrew.

And think of the birds that have sung to thee here;
Of music that charmed thee from loved ones so dear;
And, while thou art musing, let *one* little thought
Recall the old friend who these numbers hath wrought.

TO MARY.

The Old Year is dying,
The pale leaves are flying
On the wings of the whistling breeze;
The dews, that so early
Did glisten so pearly,
Into tiniest frost-crystals freeze.

The forests are sighing,
Their drapery lying
On the ground where the violets sleep;
Though mournful their losses,
The velvety mosses
Are concealed from the tempest's cold sweep;

Old Winter, so hoary,
Arrayed in the glory
Of his vestments of ice and of snow;
With pencil so chilly,
The rose on the lily
He will paint, while the fiercest winds blow.

Ah, say you I'm silly,
To speak of the lily
When it long has been withered and dead?
I speak of the flower,
The maiden's sweet dower,
That the Summer breeze stole ere it fled.

Though bleak are the mountains,
And sealed are the fountains,
And of verdure the valley is bare;
No moonlight is whiter,
No starlight is brighter,
And no skies are so blue and so fair.

Then why should you, Mary,
Of Winter be chary?
And why greet his approach with a shiver?
Though thick be the muffle
Of ripple and ruffle,
Yet beneath it still murmurs the river.

The rills, that were tinkling
With silvery sprinkling,
With the caroling bird will be still;
But the bells will be ringing,
And red lips be singing,
With the merriest voices, the liveliest trill.

And then, as to sporting,
Or old-fashioned courting,
How convenient the long evenings are!
Be careful, dear Mary!
Of such things be wary,—
Ere you know it, the chain you will wear!

TO FRANCES.

Ah, well, dear Frank, the time has come
  When we must part, perhaps forever ;
You go to seek a Western home,—
  How many ties you now must sever !

A few short months have passed away
  Since first was coiled around me
Affection's cord,—for on that day
  My Brother's wife I found thee.

I loved thee then, for he was dear,—
  No brother could be dearer ;

His heart's deep centre thou wast near,—
  No wife could e'er be nearer.

Alas, sweet Brother! he has gone,—
  We sadly saw his life-bloom wither;
The bridal day scarce passed its dawn,
  When lo! the summons, "Come up hither!"

That voice,—he knew its sweet tone well;
  It came from no unwelcome stranger;
Like music, on his heart it fell,
  And softly bade him fear no danger.

I saw thee daily o'er him bend,
  While Life's dim light was slowly waning;
And I was glad he had a friend,
  To tireless love so true remaining.

A kindred mourner has thy heart;
  Beside the Dead, thou lov'st another;

And, though I grieve with thee to part,
  I'll take thy husband for a brother.

I love you both,—so, fare ye well!
  Here, take this little, simple token;
One truthful story may it tell,—
  It is a pledge of ties unbroken.

TO A YOUNG BRIDE.

I.

Amid the throng, on Sabbath day,
  We oft have seen thy pleasant face.
Could not the stranger stay away,
  And not despoil our sacred place?
For joyed we Jenny there to meet,
Her guileless Sabbath smile to greet.

II.

I blame him not, the happy man,
  Who chanced to win so sweet a prize;
Who *chanced*, I said,—'t was in the plan
  Of One with whom our Future lies,
Who for him had a friendly thought,
And gave him Jane to bless his lot.

III.

Yes, thou wilt go; and as the vine
  In fondness clasps the sheltering tree,
Around thy husband sweetly twine
  A wife's unfailing constancy.
Should storms the sturdy Oak assail,
Cling closest in the fiercest gale.

IV.

May he thy fondest hopes fulfil,
  Unless, perchance, thy hopes are wild,—
For Lovers all are *human* still;
  And since the serpent Eve beguiled,
And Eve her Adam,—for that sin,
A different husband man has been.

V.

Remember this,—and should a frown
  E'er gather o'er his care-worn brow,
With loving glances smile it down;

And, softer than the bridal vow,
Let words of gentleness be breathed,
With grateful deeds and kisses wreathed.

VI.

And should a hasty sentence fall,
Amid the troublous cares of life,
Just think 't is *human*,—that is all,—
And let it wisely end the strife.
Curl not thy cherry lip and say,
A curse upon the bridal day.

VII.

Perhaps he 'll deem thy friend unkind,
To hint that such a cloudy day
The Future ever will unwind;
So bright appears the golden way
Young Love has pictured in his dreams,
He sees no shadows 'mid the gleams.

VIII.

Ah, well,—he ought to love thee, Jane,
  As erring mortals seldom love!
I hope so sweet will be thy reign,
  Rebellious passions ne'er will move
Disturbance in the bridal nest,
Or tumult in the manly breast.

A PRAYER.

ACROSTIC.

C elestial Spirit, Heavenly Dove!
L et down a cloud of joy and love,—
A balmy cloud, of mercies full,
R eplete with blessings for her soul.
I llume her mind with light divine,—
S weet light of Truth, serene, benign.
S ecure her heart from all its foes,
A viewless band, with train of woes.
M ove gently, Thou, upon her will;
L et Love, like evening dew, distil,
A round her path, a fragrance sweet;

N or aught withhold to make complete
D elightful union, blest accord
O f heart and life, with Christ, her Lord.
N or let her brief sojourning here
S eem only time for sigh and tear;
B ut give her Youth substantial joys,
I n place of Fashion's worthless toys.
R elieve her womanhood of cares,
T rials severe, domestic tares.
H er Age with comforts crown, and days
D elightful grant her, while she stays;
A nd down the vale her way she wends,
Y outhful again, when Life she ends.

TO MIRRIE'S VEIL.

Go, hide our Mirrie's radiant face,
  And shield it from the common gaze;
Spread o'er her features' loving grace
  Thy soft and half-concealing haze.

Defend her from the Sun's bold eye,
  When clouds refuse to screen his rays;
Nor let the dallying breezes ply,
  Unsought, their rude, familiar ways.

Should Envy burn some wretched heart,
  Or Passion kindle lurid blaze,

Thy fairy folds refuse to part,
  To e'er admit their searching rays.

Should Friendship ever turn to Hate,
  Or coldness chill some loving breast,
Protect her from the icy weight
  Of clouds that on such faces rest.

But when her soul, with raptures bright,
  Would bathe in Beauty's balmy air,
Withdraw thyself, nor shade the light
  That mountains, plains and valleys wear.

Let Summer all her wealth unfold,
  Of dewy pearl and angel flower,
That whisper, as their charms are told—
  How sweet, but transient, Beauty's power!

Aye, sweet, but transient only here,—
  In kindness sent, to tell us where

A Beauty dwells, without a fear
  Of ever, ever fading there.

As Angels once were wont to come,
  To leave on Earth a gleam of Heaven;
As on the skirt of Glory's dome,
  Serenely shines the star of Even,—

So visit us these gentle ones,
  Though transient, wielding sweeter power
Than that which streams from distant suns,
  So long of Night the golden dower.

When Autumn turns the leaves to flowers,
  To gayly robe the dying Year,
Oh, let its calm, suggestive hours
  In clear, but softened, light appear.

When Winter spreads the snowy shroud,
  To hide the sere and faded fields,

And not a whisper is allowed
  Of music that the Summer yields,—

Then let her gaze upon the scene,
  And think how soon the robe, so white,
Will melt, to let the living green
  Revive again the Spring's delight.

With such a robe we deck the Bride;
  With such we drape the sinless child,
Before the toil of Life is tried,
  With Love's fond visions all beguiled.

And thus, when Life is ended, too,
  In white we wrap the sleeping form,—
An emblem pure, the spotless snow,
  Of hopes begotten of the storm.

When Sorrow pleads with piteous moan,
  Hide not the sympathizing tear;

Reveal, with Woman's gentle tone,
   A Woman's heart, to all so dear.

If e'er a frown should shadow o'er
   Her sunny brow,—let it appear,
If Vice, disguised, should dare to pour
   Its deadly tale upon her ear.

She would not greet the staring World,
   Nor smile on all of human kind;
Yet fail not to be softly furled,
   Around her silken tresses twined.

If e'er a Love should reign supreme,
   That hath an empire all its own,—
The Real of Life's sweetest dream,—
   Her heart an undisputed throne,—

As soul with soul in union twines,
   The dearest light beneath the skies,

That ever on a mortal shines,
  Do not conceal from kindred eyes.

Aye, let it play, as sunlight plays
  Upon the ever-flowing stream,
Unchanging but as changes Day's
  Sweet dawning ray to noontide beam.

COUSIN KITTY.

Though light of step is the fairy form
  That inspires our humble ditty,
The smile is bright, and the heart is warm,
  Of our darling Cousin Kitty.

The warbling laugh, and the rippling face,
  With the repartee so witty,
Are blended sweet with the pensive grace
  Of our darling Cousin Kitty.

Though joyous e'er as wild-wood bird,
  And her changeful moods as flitty,

The hazel eyes are often blurred,
Of our darling Cousin Kitty.

Though fancies throng to her teeming mind,
As with myriads swells the city,
Yet deeper musings a welcome find
With our darling Cousin Kitty.

Whilst o'er the page, as she bendeth low.
With her ringlets dangling pretty,
Asleep are the merry dimples now,
Of our darling Cousin Kitty.

While Genius' realm is her crowded breast,
There is room for gentle Pity;
And Love is ever the cherished guest
Of our darling Cousin Kitty.

HETTIE.

As floats away the flower's bloom,
By Autumn's chilly breezes torn,
So swiftly to the silent tomb
Has Death our precious Hettie borne.

Although her Future seemed so bright,
And youthful hopes she cherished all,
Amid their gayly blended light
There glides the darkening funeral pall.

No Mother's love, or Father's prayer,
Could turn aside the dread decree ;
Nor Brothers, Sisters, weeping there,
Could make the stern Despoiler flee.

The home she loved is lonely now,
  A gloom is thrown upon our hearth;
And tears amid the shadows flow,
  Where late was heard the voice of mirth.

The arm that would have sheltered her,
  And any peril bravely dared,
No power could wield to e'en defer
  The triumph sure, by Fate prepared.

And this is Life,—with bounding heart,
  We clasp the joys of bright To-day;
To-morrow bids our bliss depart,
  And sweetest visions pass away!

Not so the Life beyond the grave,—
  Its loves and joys will live forever;
Not there will Death his banners wave,
  And loving hearts so rudely sever!

BERTHA.

Aye, darker than the raven's wing
  Are our Bertha's witching eyes;
But loving radiance do they fling,
  Where the merry dimple lies.

If only gentle thoughts betraying,
  And her lips refuse to speak;
There are ripples always playing
  In the snow upon her cheek.

If in a serious, earnest way
  She should chance to look you through,

The flash of lightning would be play
Ever afterward to you.

Perhaps a passion had been growing
In the centre of your heart,
And yet you would not have her knowing
That you felt the hidden dart.

In vain you try to draw a veil,
To conceal the naked wound;
No drapery can now avail,
For the secret has been found.

You feel as if you lived in glass,
Not a curtain for a thought;
You wish you had been made of brass,
Or of marble had been wrought.

In vain you would be very brave,
And return the naughty gaze;

You can't suppress the mounting wave,—
No, your face is all ablaze.

Your only safety now must lie
In a careless glance around,
In sudden reverence for the sky,
Or an interest in the ground.

Perhaps it would be quite as well
To attempt a hasty flight;
Perhaps a shriek would break the spell,
And relieve your sorry plight.

But never catch her eye again,
Though a smile be lurking near;
If look you must, why, venture when
She is looking through a tear.

CARRIE.

A pulpy fulness rounds her cheek,
  Like that which swells the peach ;
'T were vain a richer bloom to seek,
  Were this within your reach.

Blue-black her merry, playful e'en,
  And crystal clear are they,
While purer thought is never seen
  Round sweeter lips to play.

STELLA.

Her ample forehead white as snow,
Her eye as blue as Heaven,
Thoughts in electric currents flow,
And flash like gems of Even.

EFFOGENE.

My darling little Effogene,
  How came your eyes to be so blue?
Say, came their color from the sky,
  Or did an Angel look at you?

Now promise me, my little Bird,
  Those eyes shall always loving be;
That bitter feeling, bitter thought,
  Shall never mar their purity.

How came your lips to be so red?
  What flower lent its rosy hue?

And when you kissed it, did it die,
  And give its fragrance all to you?

May Malice never blister them,
  Nor wicked Passion turn them white;
May words of kindness keep them sweet,
  Nor circling smiles e'er take their flight.

MY SCHOLAR.

She does her duty quietly,
  Without parade or show;
Preserving sweet simplicity,
  Her busy moments flow.

I love to watch the play of thought,
  When she recites her task;
And seldom is she careless caught,
  Unheeding what I ask.

She turns away her flashing eyes,
  And penetrates her theme;

The answer to her red lip flies,
  And brings a happy gleam.

If all the path of Life she treads
  As promptly as at school,
Whoever dark-eyed Katy weds
  Will find his cup is full.

She will not fail to act her part
  In all the cares of Life,
And with her true and loving heart
  Will make, why, what a wife!

MY ISLAND HOME.

A SONG.

Like pearls on the bosom of Beauty pressed,
Like lilies that float on the water's breast,
Gleams from the Lake my lovely Home,
From its dimpled waves, my Island Home.

Let others go to the gorgeous West,
And others the land by the Bondman dressed;
O let me never, O never roam,
While I may dwell in my Island Home.

Let others fly from our crystal Lake,
And tire of the music its billows make;

Oh, let me gaze on their silvery foam,
As they break on the shores of my Island Home.

Let others go to the city proud,
Inhaling the breath of its panting crowd;
Oh, let me breathe the fragrant bloom,
And bathe in the air of my Island Home.

Let others go to the village bright,
And gayly bask in its brilliant light;
Oh, let me hie to the humble dome,
Where the loved resort, of my Island Home.

If any sigh for a sweet repose,
A blest retreat from the great World's woes,
Oh, let them hither, Oh, hither come,
And taste the joys of my Island Home.

LAKE CHAMPLAIN.

A SONG.

Let others sing of the deep blue sea,
With its mountain waves, and its coral groves;
Be mine the rapture to sing of thee,
Around whose shores are our early loves.

Let others sing of the crystal stream,
That sweetly murmurs along the dell;
Or merry rills that in gladness seem
To hasten hither, with thee to dwell.

Around our Isle do thy waters gleam,
With morning's blush and the evening's glow,
Or moonlight's silvery, floating beam,
When weary breezes refuse to blow.

Whene'er thy bosom is calm and bright,
  We love to gaze on the smooth expanse;
And when thy billows are crested white,
  What joy to look at their foamy dance!

The flood-worn pebble we love to throw,
  And see it bound o'er thy glassy breast,
And watch the ripples that circling flow
  Around the beach, by the waves caressed.

Thy music swells with the rising breeze,
  With the storm-howl chimes, and the tempest's roar,
And softly blends with the whispering trees,
  As soon as the rage of the wind is o'er.

We love to list to the boatman's song,
  As, keeping time with the dripping oar,
He swiftly urges his skiff along,
  And wakes the ripples that slept before.

A WELCOME.

Welcome to our Island Home,
Now that balmy Spring has come;
Welcome to its waters bright,
Gleaming in the vernal light.

Listen to the merry waves,
Murmuring o'er each other's graves:
Bound in icy chains no more,
Hear them lash the laughing shore.

When the winds are all asleep,
See how lovingly they creep,

On the bosom they have lapped,
In a silver mantle wrapped.

See the vessel's snowy sail
Fly before the rushing gale,
Or curvetting to elude,
With another's will endued.

Hear the steamers, as they plow,
Dash the billows from the prow;
See their long and swelling trail,
Floating lightly, like a veil.

Welcome to our evergreens,
Minding thee of mountain scenes,
Fringes of the rocky bound,
Skirting all the Island 'round.

Welcome to the grasses sweet,
Fearless now of Winter sleet,

Freshly springing from the ground,
Late so soberly embrowned.

Welcome to the early flowers,
Prelude of the Summer hours,
Lifting up their faces fair,
Careless of the chilly air.

Welcome to the harmonies,
Floating sweetly in the breeze,—
Voices of awakened loves,
Gushing from the tuneful groves.

THE DESERTED HOME.

I.

The old deserted Home!
Oh, who that once could fondly claim
A spot by that endearing name,
Wherever he may roam,
But oft will turn,
With tears that burn,
His eyes to that familiar place,
Abandoned now by all his race!

II.

Oh, I remember well,
The snow-white House, with dark green blinds,
The path that through the door-yard winds,

The trees whose shadows fell
O'er flowering bush,
Softening the blush
Of roses bright, that Mother's care
Had planted, kept and nourished there.

III.

My Mother loved her flowers;
They were the gentle counterpart
Of those that bloomed within her heart.
Oh, sweet the quiet hours
She snatched from toil,
And Life's turmoil,
With calm communing both to bless
With sweet exchange of loveliness.

IV.

Oh, yes, the well is there,
Wherein the mossy bucket hung,
Which cooled our lips when we were young,

And thither did repair;
And neighing Nell,
And bright-eyed Belle,
Who watched the dripping bucket too,
Ready to drink when we were through.

V.

The dear old fruit trees bend
Their loaded branches to the ground;
The clustering vines are creeping round,
And sweet enchantment lend;
The garden plot,
Delightful spot!
Within the homely picket fence,
Of treasures rich the sure defence.

VI.

Why do I linger here,
When opens wide the ancient door,
Through which so oft we passed before?

Why starts the scalding tear?
Alas, alas!
Why should I pass
That threshold door, and, weeping, gaze,
On relics sad of other days?

VII.

Right by, the sacred hearth
Where Father used to sit I see,
Where daily, too, he bent the knee,
And soared away from earth
In such a prayer,
The very air
Seemed hallowed, while he bowed
And pure devotion breathed aloud.

VIII.

And there the table stood,
Around which gathered all the band
Of loved ones,—spread by Mother's hand

With such delicious food
As only she,
It seemed to me,
Of all the world, could e'er prepare
For us who daily feasted there.

IX.

And *there* my bed was made,
Between whose sheets we nightly crept,
Brother and I, and sweetly slept,
Our prayer devoutly said.
Oh, sweet the bliss
Of good-night kiss,
That she, so kind, so good, so meek,
Our Mother, left upon our cheek.

X.

Dear old deserted Home,
Farewell! I cannot longer stay.
Since all I loved are far away,

Oh, let me longer roam;
Nor look again,
With throbbing brain,
Upon this spot, so lonely now.
A long farewell I sadly bow!

OUR GRAVE-YARD.

Drawn by the sweet repose of tranquil Night,
I have come out to breathe this dewy air.
The Moon's broad disc lies brightly on the sky,
And floods the world with such a wealth of light,
That all things seem immersed in silver waves.
The Stars are faintly glimmering through this depth
Of brightness, save the few that shine along
The mountain-girt horizon, or appear
Within the broken folds of floating clouds.
The winds are all asleep, and silence reigns,
And all the forms of busy, active life are hushed.
The dew is gathering on these turfy mounds;

The white stones glitter in the silver flood,
As, motionless, they lean above the graves.
The grey old mossy monuments alone
Refuse to smile, and seem to sleep with those
Whose names they long have faithful borne,—
Like aged men, outliving all their kin,
Whose sympathies refuse to blend with those
Of strangers, who have come since they have passed
Away, with whom they mingled in their youth.
Such quiet reigns, so still the fragrant air,
Steeped in this liquid silver, that it seems
As if the World was dead, and I alone
Survive, and walk amid these crowded graves,
To find a spot where I may also sleep.
What multitudes are here, in this small space,
Who once could claim broad acres as their own,
And died unsatisfied, who yet have lain,
These many years, within these narrow beds!
How many happy homes have yielded up
Their sweetest treasures to be buried here!

How many brave, ambitious men have left,
Reluctantly, the busy stage of Life,
To swell the crowd that yearly gathers here!
How many reverend forms of those we loved,
And fondly, vainly wished might never die,
Have we been forced to sadly bring,
And lay them by the side of those they helped
To bury. Boys, and girls, and little babes,
Are here,—the ever-varying forms of graves,
From that wherein the infant lies, to those
Betokening lofty stature, indicate
That all, of every age and class, must pay
Their due proportion of the general debt.
How many faces are there buried here,
Familiar even unto me, although
So short a time has passed since they to me
Were strangers. Yes, I seem to see them all:
Their smiles, their tears, their laughter, and their songs,
With all their pleasant tones of kind discourse,
Discourse beside their dear, familiar hearths,

And scenes around my own, come rushing on
Th' electric wires of faithful Memory!

Beneath that stone a Father lies, and there
A Mother,—mine by virtue of the ties
Which kindness, never faltering, surely binds.
And there an early Friend, who, in the prime
Of youthful, joyous life, God took away.
I well remember that sweet smile of his,
Alas! and that last, trembling, dying gaze!
When, grasping firm a hand of each of us,
His friend's, and *hers*, he must have loved so well,
He gave the sad farewell, and waited for the pang
That soon released him!

There, almost complete,
A circle slumbers, that, a few years since,
Were floating on the tide of prosperous seas,—
All here but one! their wealth, their homes, the source
Of others' joys, the sphere of others' toil.

These grave-stones do not tell whose mouldering dust
Most precious is ; no doubt there are beneath
These nameless mounds, whose cherished memories
Are held most dear, and sacredly enshrined.
The polish shaft, and rude, unsculptured stone,
Bears a like record of the loved and lost.

That low and humble stone,—the first one raised
Within this yard, that bears a name by most
Forgotten,—I have seen an old man stand
Trembling beside it, sobbing like a child,
Because there rested the dear form of her
Whose love was the sweet blossom of his youth.
He lingers still, and, drawing near the verge
Of ninety years, he asks one only boon,—
That we should lay him by the side of her
Who was his first and dearest.

When a child,
With startled interest, I was wont to hear

My Father tell of the Black Snake, and how,
In wanton recklessness, the smugglers slew
Their fellows, who, obedient to the law,
Were seeking to enforce its honest claims.
How Dean was hung, while he, whose guilty hand
Sent to untimely graves his countrymen,
Was suffered still to live.

I little dreamed
That I should ever see him;—but there came
A grey-haired stranger to our Isle,
Who seemed to have a burden on his soul.
He wore a troubled look;—his features seemed
As moulded by some life-worn grief.—Remorse
Had furrowed deep his cheek,—his vacant eyes
Seemed to be looking at some olden scene,
That held him with unyielding grasp.
A lonely man, he moved along our streets
As if he recognized no kindred heart
Among his fellow-men, though none reproached

Him now, and none withheld kind words or deeds.
One day they told me he was dead; and soon
We gathered at the House of Prayer, and thence
We bore him to his grave,—and there he lies,
Without a stone to mark the place, or tell
The passing stranger that a man of blood,
A man-slayer, sleeps among our precious dead.

And there reposes one, who claimed to be
One of Napoleon's brave Imperial Guard.
Far from his country, and his Fathers' graves,
He sleeps, while he for whom he bared his breast
Is almost worshipped, and his dust, enshrined,
Attracts a Nation's proud idolatry.
This stranger had a soldier's haughty mien;
His frame was lofty, massive, and his eyes,
So fierce, would wake a shudder when we met
Their fearful gaze.

The Moon is shining still;
These graves are silent, but————

www.ingramcontent.com/pod-product-compliance
Lightning Source LLC
Chambersburg PA
CBHW031359270326
41929CB00010BA/1249

* 9 7 8 3 7 4 4 7 1 0 7 2 5 *